LIGHTS IN THE NIGHT

True Stories of Unexplained Encounters

PASTOR JOE LIGHTHALL

Copyright © 2025 by Joe Lighthall

All rights reserved.

No part of this book may be reproduced, stored in a retrieval system, or transmitted in any form or by any means—electronic, mechanical, photocopying, recording, or otherwise—without the prior written permission of the publisher, except for brief quotations in critical reviews or articles.

ISBN 978-1-918219-07-4

First Edition: 2025

Published by: Cosmic Jive Publishing
www.cosmicjivepublishing.com

Disclaimer: The views expressed in this book are solely those of the author and do not necessarily reflect the official policy or position of the publisher.

For permissions and inquiries, contact: info@cosmicjivepublishing.com

About the Author

Joe Lighthall has served as a pastor in the American Midwest for many years. Before that, he worked as a missionary in Eastern Europe, traveling behind the Iron Curtain during the Cold War. Those years included carrying Bibles across borders where the Scriptures were forbidden, meeting with believers in hidden house churches, and witnessing first-hand how faith endured under persecution.

Since the 1970s, Pastor Joe has gathered stories of encounters with angels—accounts that come from many nations, cultures, and generations. His approach has always been both pastoral and cautious: he listens carefully, verifies what he can, and measures every testimony against Scripture and sober Christian discernment. His purpose has never been to sensationalize, but to encourage believers who wonder whether God still breaks into ordinary lives.

Over time, he collected far more stories than a single volume could hold. Three have been punished to date and additional books of angel testimonies—Volume 4 and beyond—are planned, along with a separate series on miracles: healings, provisions, and moments of divine intervention that reveal the same faithful God at work.

However, a third category of accounts gradually demanded attention: stories commonly described today as **"UFO encounters."**

Pastor Joe eventually realized that many of these testimonies carry the same hallmarks as biblical angel encounters—messages, protection, warnings, overwhelming peace, transformative experiences, and fruit that points people toward God. In other words, many of these so-called "UFO encounters" (note, he does not say all), may well be angelic encounters described through the lens of modern language and technology.

If that is true, then why not simply merge them with the other angel stories?

The answer is pastoral. Many people who have had these experiences feel **isolated, misunderstood, or even mocked—especially in Christian settings.** Some are afraid to speak to a pastor at all. Others would never pick up a book labeled "angel stories," assuming it has nothing to do with what they saw or experienced. At the same time, many believers who appreciate angel testimonies are uneasy with modern UFO terminology. Putting the accounts together would risk losing both groups.

By giving these stories their own series, Pastor Joe creates a safe and thoughtful space—free from the sensationalism that often surrounds the subject—where experiencers can be heard without ridicule and where Christians can examine these events without fear or embarrassment. The separation also makes it clear that while these encounters may indeed be angelic in nature, the cultural context surrounding them is unique and requires sensitive, careful handling.

Pastor Joe's hope is simple: that no matter how unusual or unexpected these testimonies may appear, readers will come to see that God is not distant—and that His messengers can still meet people in ways that defy expectation, whether described in ancient terms or through the language of the modern sky.

Author's Note on Testimonies & Confidentiality

The stories in this book are true accounts. While many individuals boldly embrace their testimonies and are unashamed to be named, others—such as family members, friends, or those connected to these events—have not given explicit permission to be identified. To respect their privacy, certain names, locations and identifying details have been changed. However, the divine encounters and spiritual truths <u>remain unchanged.</u>

Every effort has been made to present these testimonies with accuracy and respect. If any story unintended resembles a reader's personal experience without direct acknowledgment, it is entirely coincidental.

INTRODUCTION
When Heaven Flies

THERE ARE MOMENTS when the ordinary world cracks open, just slightly, and we glimpse something that doesn't fit our categories. A light that moves wrong. A presence that defies physics. An encounter that leaves us changed, uncertain whether to speak of it or bury it deep.

For decades, I have listened to such stories. As a pastor and former missionary behind the Iron Curtain, I learned that extraordinary experiences don't respect our neat theological boxes. I've sat across from engineers, teachers, farmers, pilots, and mothers—people of sound mind and steady faith—who have seen things on the earth that defy explanation. I've written about some of these experiences in my books on angels.

Many of these folks stayed silent for years. Some still do. It's odd that a church that claims to believe in the supernatural often struggles with belief when an ordinary member of their flock claims an extraordinary experience. Many people who experience the divine find themselves suddenly put into a "questionable" category and disbelieved by the people who should rejoice and wonder with them.

But there are also those believers who have seen things in the *sky*. And these people struggle the most, especially when Christian. In the church and outside of it.

The phenomenon we call "UFOs" carries baggage. Mention it in church and watch the room divide: some roll their eyes at "conspiracy theories," others whisper about demons, and a few lean forward with stories they've never dared share publicly. Meanwhile, secular culture has claimed the entire conversation, filling it with aliens, government cover-ups, and science fiction.

But what if we've been asking the wrong questions?

What if some of these encounters—not all, but some—are something the ancient world would have recognized immediately? What if the lights in the sky, the impossible movements, the sense of presence and protection, are not as foreign to Scripture as we assume?

The prophet Ezekiel saw wheels within wheels, full of eyes, moving with intelligence that defied comprehension (Ezekiel 1:16-21). The Magi followed a star that moved with purpose, guiding them precisely to Bethlehem (Matthew 2:9-10). Throughout Scripture, divine messengers appear in ways that overwhelm human perception—in fire, in clouds, in forms that inspire both terror and awe.

So when a faithful Christian pilot encounters lights that manoeuvre impossibly, or a praying farmer sees luminous figures over his fields, or a missionary witnesses phenomena that defy natural law—should we automatically dismiss it? Label it demonic? Or might we be encountering something the biblical writers would have called "angels of the Lord"?

This book doesn't claim to have all the answers. I write with humility, knowing that much remains mystery. The tension many believers feel around this subject is real and understandable. We're caught between multiple fears: fear of being deceived by Satan (who can masquerade as an angel of light), fear of seeming gullible or unstable, fear of contradicting Scripture, fear of opening ourselves to the occult.

These concerns are entirely valid. Scripture instructs us to "test the spirits" (1 John 4:1) precisely because not everything that appears supernatural is from God. (And to be clear, I'm not suggesting that every unidentified light in the sky is "supernatural" in the usual sense—even if such lights were produced by craft not of this world, they could still be natural phenomena.) The spiritual realm is active, complex, and includes forces hostile to the Christian faith. Discernment isn't optional—it's essential.

But here's what troubles me: in our rightful caution about deception, many Christians have swung to the opposite extreme. We've become so afraid of being fooled that we automatically dismiss anything unexplained. We've created an unwritten rule: if you can't explain it naturally, and it doesn't fit our narrow conception of how God works, it must be either delusion or demonic.

This reactionary skepticism doesn't match Scripture's own treatment of mystery. The Bible is full of encounters that awed witnesses but defied their understanding. Ezekiel struggled to describe what he saw, using phrases like "the appearance of the likeness" because language failed him (Ezekiel 1:26-28).

The early church fathers understood this tension. They wrote extensively about angels, demons, and spiritual realities while maintaining rigorous discernment. They didn't assume every vision was divine, but neither did they dismiss the supernatural realm as irrelevant or inactive. They lived both cautious and open, both discerning and expectant.

We've lost that balance. Modern churchianity has largely adopted a cessationist mindset even when it doesn't formally hold cessationist theology. We believe God *could* do miraculous things, but we don't really *expect* Him to—and we're suspicious of anyone who claims He has.

This creates a problem for sincere believers who've experienced something extraordinary. A pilot who encounters lights performing maneuvers that violate physics. A fisherman guided to safety through dense fog. A farmer whose crops are spared in ways that defy agricultural science. These people aren't seeking attention. They're not mentally unstable. They're not dabbling in the occult. They're not trying to sell conferences or merch. They're simply trying to reconcile what they witnessed with their faith.

Too often, the church responds with silence, discomfort, or outright dismissal. We'd rather these experiences didn't happen because they're messy, they don't fit our systematic theologies, and they require us to acknowledge that God's ways might exceed our categories.

Then there's a category of Christian who insist every single "alien" encounter is demonic and if one says the Lord's prayer enough times, or invokes the name of Jesus, the aliens will disappear on command.

I've collected these five accounts because they share something remarkable: people whose encounters left them not traumatized, but blessed. Not confused, but closer to

God. Not fearful, but filled with wonder at the vastness of creation. These aren't the marks of demonic deception or mental breakdown. They're the marks of genuine encounters with the holy.

Yes, discernment matters. I cannot emphasize this enough. Not every unexplained phenomenon is angelic. Some may be natural events we don't yet understand. Some may be human technology, classified or experimental. And yes, some may be deceptive—spiritual realities that masquerade as beneficial but ultimately lead away from Christ.

Scripture gives us tests for discernment:

- Does the experience acknowledge Jesus Christ as Lord come in the flesh? (1 John 4:2-3)
- Does it produce good fruit—love, peace, patience, kindness? (Galatians 5:22-23)
- Does it lead toward God or away from Him? (Matthew 7:16-20)
- Does it align with God's character as revealed in Scripture?
- Does it create dependence on the experience itself, or point beyond to God?

By these measures, the encounters in this book pass. But I'm not asking you to simply accept my assessment. I'm asking you to read carefully, think critically, pCarl for wisdom, and apply biblical discernment yourself.

I'm also asking you to remain open to the possibility that angels—if they exist and remain active (which Scripture affirms)—might not always appear in the forms we expect. The Bible describes angels as men (Genesis 18-19), as fire (Exodus 3:2), as beings so overwhelming that witnesses fall down in terror (Daniel 10:5-9), and as wheels within wheels covered in eyes (Ezekiel 1).

Why would we assume angels must always appear as winged humans in white robes? That's Renaissance art, not biblical description. The actual biblical portrayals are often stranger, more diverse, and yes—sometimes technological in appearance to modern eyes.

Consider: if angels are spiritual beings with power over physical matter, if they can appear and disappear at will, if they can move at speeds beyond human comprehension, if they radiate light and manipulate energy—wouldn't that look technological to us? Wouldn't we reach for technological metaphors to describe what we're seeing?

Ezekiel saw wheels, structures, coordinated movements that his agricultural society could only describe in mechanical terms. If he saw the same thing today, might he describe it differently? Might it sound like a UFO report?

I'm not claiming all UFOs are angels. I'm suggesting we shouldn't automatically assume they're not, especially when the encounter bears good fruit and leads toward God rather than away from Him.

The people in these pages didn't go seeking strange experiences. They were simply living their lives—praying, working, serving God—when heaven intersected with earth in ways that challenged everything they thought they knew. Their stories remind us that God's creation is vaster, stranger, and more magnificent than our Sunday school

Lights in the Sky

lessons suggested.

Many struggle with this topic because it sits at the intersection of faith and mystery, certainty and humility, caution and openness. We want clear answers. We want to know definitively whether these phenomena are angelic, natural, or deceptive. But perhaps God allows some mystery to remain precisely because it requires us to exercise both faith and discernment, to hold tension without collapsing it into easy answers.

C.S. Lewis explored this in his Space Trilogy, suggesting that what medieval people called angels and modern people call aliens might point to the same realities viewed through different cultural lenses. Lewis wasn't claiming all UFOs are angels—he was noting that our neat categories of "natural" and "supernatural" might be less clear than we assume.

Lewis wrote in *Miracles*: "There is no reason to suppose that the frontiers between [the natural and supernatural] are stiff and fast, or that we know exactly where they run."

If spiritual beings can interact with physical reality, if angels can manipulate matter and energy, then the boundary between "spiritual" and "technological" becomes fuzzy.

So I invite you to read with an open mind and a discerning heart. Don't believe everything. But don't dismiss everything either. Test the spirits. Examine the fruit. Ask whether these accounts lead toward Christ or away from Him. Consider whether the witnesses demonstrate wisdom, humility, and continued faithfulness—or whether they've become obsessed, proud, or disconnected from biblical truth. At the same time, remember David and Solomon—men who truly encountered the living God, yet still fell. Their stories remind us that discernment is more complex than simply evaluating outward fruit.

The stories that follow are true, documented as carefully as possible, and shared with the prayer that they might expand your vision of what's possible when heaven touches earth. Some readers will remain skeptical—that's fine. Skepticism has its place. Others will recognize echoes of their own experiences and feel less alone. That's the primary goal: to create space for honest testimony, biblical reflection, and community discernment.

Because if angels still walk among us—if they move through our skies with purposes we can barely comprehend—then perhaps the lights we've been taught to fear are actually invitations to wonder.

The heavens declare the glory of God, the psalmist wrote (Psalm 19:1). Perhaps they still do—in ways that would make Ezekiel nod with recognition and our modern categories of "alien" or "angel" seem far too small.

Welcome to the edge of mystery.

TESTIMONY 1:
The Pilot's Light

CARL PETERSON grew up beneath the broad skies of northern Oklahoma, where the horizon seemed endless and thunderheads rolled like cathedrals of vapor. His father, a quiet man of deep faith, would point upward during evening walks and quote Psalm 19:1: "The heavens declare the glory of God." For young Carl, those words became a lens through which he viewed the world.

The Peterson farm sat on land that had been in the family for three generations. Carl's grandfather had homesteaded it in the 1920s, building the farmhouse that still stood—weathered but solid—on a slight rise overlooking wheat fields that stretched to the horizon. The land taught lessons about patience, perseverance, and trust. You planted in faith, tended carefully, and hoped for rain. The outcome was never entirely in your hands.

Carl's father extended that agricultural faith to all of life. He saw God's hand in the wheat's growth, in the storms that watered it, in the harvest that sustained them. And he saw it in the sky—that vast Oklahoma sky that could turn from crystalline blue to roiling purple in the span of an hour, that displayed storms and sunsets with equal drama, that seemed to press God's grandeur into every person who looked up.

Young Carl absorbed these lessons. He'd lie in the grass on summer evenings, watching the stars emerge one by one, feeling simultaneously insignificant and precious—a small boy under an infinite sky, yet known and loved by the One who made it all. Those quiet moments shaped his soul more than any sermon ever would.

When high school ended, Carl knew he didn't want to farm. He loved the land, but his eyes kept lifting skyward. He wanted to fly. His parents, practical people who'd struggled through drought and depression, worried about the expense of flight school. But they also believed in following where God led, so they helped him find a way.

Carl worked construction summers, saved every penny, and enrolled in a flight program at a regional college. He soloed on his twentieth birthday—a moment he'd later describe as transcendent, the earth falling away beneath him, the sky opening in invitation. Flying wasn't just technical skill; it was communion with the vastness he'd always loved.

The Air Force recruited him straight out of college. Still in his twenties, he was flying combat missions over hostile territory, navigating by stars when electronics failed, trusting instruments and instincts in equal measure. The military sharpened his skills but couldn't diminish his sense of wonder. Even in war zones, he'd find moments to look up and remember his father's words: *The heavens declare the glory of God.*

By 1996, Carl was an experienced pilot with hundreds of hours logged, most of them routine. Gulf patrols were monotonous—long stretches of darkness broken only by instrument checks and occasional radio chatter. The danger was minimal; the boredom, substantial.

Which is why the night of April 13th stood out so starkly.

It was approximately 0200 hours. Carl was flying patrol with his wingman, Lieutenant Paul Reed, maintaining standard altitude and heading. The Gulf stretched black and featureless below. Above, stars blazed with the clarity possible only far from land-based light pollution.

Carl had been scanning the horizon mechanically, mind half on the flight plan, half on the letter he'd write to his wife when he landed.

Then Lt. Reed's voice cracked through the radio, tight with tension: "Peterson, you seeing that? Two o'clock, approximately twenty miles, low altitude."

Carl's eyes snapped to the indicated position. At first, he saw nothing. Then—there. A faint glow on the horizon, distinguishable from stars only by its movement. As he watched, it grew brighter, closer.

"I've got it," Carl confirmed, his pulse quickening. "Checking radar."

The radar scope was clean. No returns, no contacts. Carl cycled through frequencies, checked his instruments. Everything functioned normally. Yet visually, something was definitely there—and approaching fast.

"I've got nothing on instruments," Lt. Reed reported. "But visual confirmation. It's... holy smoke, what on earth is that?"

The object resolved as it approached. Not a conventional aircraft—Carl knew every silhouette in the military inventory, both friendly and hostile. This was roughly oval, glowing with a golden-white luminescence that seemed to emanate from within rather than reflecting external light. It had no wings. No tail. No visible means of propulsion.

It hovered off Carl's starboard side, matching his speed and altitude perfectly.

Carl's training kicked in. He cycled through the identification protocols: attempt radio contact, prepare defensive measures if needed, maintain situational awareness. But even as his hands moved through the practiced motions, his mind struggled to process what his eyes reported.

"Unidentified aircraft, this is US Navy patrol November-Seven-Three, please identify yourself." Carl's voice was steady despite his racing heart.

No response. The object continued hovering, pulsing gently.

"Should we break off?" Reed asked. "I can request backup—"

"Hold position," Carl said. Something in his gut—call it intuition, call it something else—told him there was no threat here. The object's behavior wasn't aggressive. It was... observant. Almost curious.

Then it moved.

Not gradually. Not with the acceleration curve of any known aircraft. It simply *was* there, then it *was* approximately three miles away, and then it *was* directly ahead, having covered the distance in what Carl's mind registered as instantaneous. His body jerked against the harness, adrenaline flooding his system, even as his rational mind insisted that what he'd just seen was impossible.

The object hovered ahead of them, slightly above their altitude. Carl could see details now in the moonlight: even more visible because of the object's glow. The surface wasn't solid but seemed to shift like liquid light, patterns rippling across it in waves. The glow intensified briefly, then dimmed, intensified again—not randomly, but rhythmically. Like breathing. Like something alive.

"I'm seeing... movement that's not possible," Reed said, his voice strained. "The G-forces alone should have—"

"I know," Carl kept his aircraft steady, eyes locked on the phenomenon ahead. His instruments still showed nothing. Radar remained clean. But visually, undeniably, something was there.

The object began moving again, this time in a pattern: right angle turn upward (impossible), sudden stop (equally impossible), sideways drift (violating every principle of aerodynamics), then a spiral descent that should have created visible thrust or disturbance but didn't. It moved like thought made visible, like consciousness directing energy without mechanical intermediation.

Carl found himself forgetting to be afraid. The movements, while impossible, weren't erratic. They were... beautiful. Precise. Almost playful, like a dancer demonstrating skill, or a teacher showing students what's possible.

For perhaps ten minutes—though time felt strange, elastic—the object performed its aerial ballet. Carl and his lieutenant watched, occasionally reporting position and observations to each other but mostly silent, witnessing something that exceeded their categories.

Then, as suddenly as it began, it ended. The object tilted (though it had no visible top or bottom to tilt), pulsed one final time with increased brilliance, and shot straight up.

Carl tracked it with his eyes: five hundred feet, a thousand, five thousand—altitude markers that became meaningless as the object accelerated beyond anything he could follow. Then it was simply gone, leaving only stars and the familiar darkness.

"Did that just…" Reed's voice trailed off.

"Yeah," Carl said. "It did."

The men completed their patrol in near silence, each processing privately what they'd witnessed. When they landed, their debriefing was perfunctory. The commanding officer took their report, made notes, asked if they'd been fatigued or experienced equipment malfunction. When they insisted everything had functioned normally and yes, they both saw it, he sighed and filed the report as "unidentified aerial phenomenon, no threat determined."

Carl knew that report would disappear into classified files, never to be discussed officially again. But he couldn't make it disappear from his memory. That night, lying in his bunk while others slept, he replayed every moment: the glow, the movements, the sense of being observed by something with clear intelligence.

And he remembered something else—a detail his conscious mind had noted but not fully processed in the moment. When the object had hovered closest, when he'd looked directly at it, he'd felt something. Not fear, though fear would have been rational. Not confusion, though confusion would have been understandable.

He'd felt peace.

Deep, penetrating peace, the kind he'd only experienced a few times in his life: during his baptism, on his wedding day, the night his first child was born. Moments when the ordinary world seemed to thin and he sensed the presence of something vast and loving and utterly beyond him.

The object—whatever it was—had radiated that same peace. And Carl trained to assess threats and maintain combat readiness, had instinctively recognized it as benign. More than benign: protective, even.

He thought of his father's words: *The heavens declare the glory of God.* He thought of Ezekiel's wheels within wheels. He thought of the star that guided the Magi—a star that, according to Matthew's account, moved and stopped with obvious intelligence (Matthew 2:9).

What if those ancient accounts weren't metaphorical? What if the biblical writers were describing real phenomena, just like he'd seen tonight? What if angels—or whatever heaven sends to accomplish its purposes—sometimes appear in forms that look more technological than traditional, more luminous than anthropomorphic?

Carl didn't claim to know. But lying there in the dark, feeling the subtle rock of the ship, listening to the breathing of fellow pilots around him, he couldn't shake the conviction that he'd encountered something holy. Something that belonged to God's realm, not humanity's. Something that had appeared, observed, and departed, leaving him not harmed but strangely blessed.

* * *

In the days that followed, Carl said nothing to his fellow pilots beyond what was recorded in the official report. The debrief was handled by someone who, Carl could tell, had heard stories like this before—and who believed both him and Reed without hesitation. It confirmed what pilots only whispered about in their own circles: that the strange encounters spoken of since the Foo Fighters of World War II were still happening today.

The incident became classified—not dramatically so, but enough that casual discussion was discouraged. Lt. Reed, his wingman, caught his eye occasionally with an expression that said *we know what we saw*, but they didn't speak of it.

Carl tried to return to normal. He flew routine patrols, maintained his aircraft, wrote letters home to his wife, Laura. But the encounter had cracked something open in him, created a space where questions could form that he'd never allowed before.

He'd grown up with faith, attended church faithfully, accepted the Bible as true. But it had all been somewhat abstract—doctrines to believe, stories from ancient times, a framework for living morally. He'd never doubted it, but he'd never really *encountered* it either. Faith was inheritance, habit, good honest living, background noise to a life focused on flying and family.

Now, suddenly, faith felt urgent. The object he'd seen—the *being*, because he was increasingly convinced it had been alive somehow—had manifested in physical space, following physical (if impossible) laws, present to his senses in undeniable ways. If that was real, if spiritual realities could break into material existence like that, then faith wasn't just intellectual assent. It was recognition of a world larger and stranger than the one he navigated by instruments.

He started reading his Bible differently. Before, he'd read

dutifully, looking for moral guidance or inspirational verses. Now he read like an investigator, searching for precedents, for patterns of divine intervention, for descriptions of encounters that might shed light on his own.

He found them everywhere.

Genesis 28: Jacob sleeping in the wilderness, seeing a stairway to heaven with angels ascending and descending. Not metaphor—Jacob woke terrified, declaring *"this is none other than the house of God"* (v. 17). Jacob had encountered something real.

Judges 6: An angel appearing to Gideon, fire consuming an offering, the angel vanishing. Gideon's response: building an altar, recognizing he'd seen something beyond normal experience.

Exodus 3: Moses and the burning bush, flames that didn't consume, a voice from the fire. Phenomenon and presence combined, compelling enough that Moses hid his face in fear.

2 Kings 2: Elijah taken up in a whirlwind, chariots and horses of fire. Elisha witnessing it, tearing his clothes, recognizing he'd seen the powers of heaven made visible.

And most relevantly, Ezekiel 1: The entire chapter describing wheels within wheels, living creatures, fire moving between them, a vast expanse gleaming like crystal. Ezekiel struggled with language, using "like" and "as if" and "appearance of" because what he witnessed exceeded vocabulary. At the end, he could only say: "This was the appearance of the likeness of the glory of the Lord" (v. 28).

Carl read that chapter repeatedly, struck by how technological Ezekiel's description sounded: wheels, structures, coordinated movement, gleaming surfaces. If Ezekiel saw the same kind of phenomenon Carl had witnessed, wouldn't he describe it in the only technical language he knew—wheels, fire, metalwork?

The star that guided the Magi (Matthew 2:9-10) became another touchstone. Stars don't stop over specific locations. They don't move independently of celestial mechanics. Whatever the Magi followed wasn't a normal astronomical body—it was something that moved with intelligence and purpose, leading them precisely to where Christ lay.

Could that have been the same kind of phenomenon Carl witnessed? A manifestation of divine power taking a form—light, movement, purpose—that served God's goals?

Carl didn't share these reflections with anyone. He knew how they'd sound: pilot sees UFO, starts interpreting Bible through conspiracy lens, next thing you know he's on TV claiming aliens built the pyramids. He wasn't claiming any such thing. He was simply trying to reconcile his experience with his faith, and finding that Scripture actually provided more framework for it than he'd expected.

But the questions weighed on him. During flights, his mind would wander back to that night. During chapel services on the carrier, he'd find himself distracted, wondering if any other people in the room had seen similar things and stayed silent like him.

The weight of unshared experience is particular. It isolates. When you've witnessed something extraordinary that others dismiss or can't comprehend, you carry it alone, and it shapes you in ways visible only to yourself. Carl felt himself changing—becoming more contemplative, more attuned to mystery, less certain about the clear categories he'd once taken for granted.

Three months after the encounter, his deployment ended. He returned to the States, to Laura and their small home near the base. The first night back, after their daughter was asleep, Laura looked at him across the dinner table and said, "Something happened out there."

It wasn't a question.

Carl met her eyes. They'd been married eight years. She knew him too well for evasion. "Yeah," he said quietly. "Something did."

He told her everything. The object, the movements, the peace he'd felt, the questions that had haunted him since. He expected skepticism, concern about his mental state, or worse—fear that he was losing his grip on reality.

Instead, Laura reached across the table and took his hands. "You think it was an angel?"

"I don't know," Carl admitted. "I keep thinking about Ezekiel, about the star the wise men followed. If those were real—actually real, not just spiritual metaphors—then they looked pretty strange too. Wheels in wheels. A star that moves and stops. Why shouldn't angels look like lights that move impossibly?"

Laura considered this. "My grandmother used to say angels come in whatever form serves God's purpose. Sometimes people, sometimes dreams, sometimes signs we almost miss. Maybe sometimes lights in the sky."

They talked until well past midnight—about faith and mystery, about Scripture's strange accounts, about how to hold certainty and unknowing in the same hand. Laura

25

shared that her own grandmother had claimed to see strange lights during prayer, back in the 1940s - before Roswell a few months after, before anyone talked about UFOs. She'd called them "God's messengers" and never questioned what they were beyond that.

"Maybe we've made it too complicated," Laura suggested. "Ancient people saw lights, strange phenomena, beings that didn't fit normal categories. They said 'angel' or 'messenger of God' and accepted the mystery. We see the same things and immediately start debating alien civilizations versus demonic deception, as if those are the only options."

"So what do I do with this?" Carl asked. "I can't unknow what I saw. It's there every time I fly, every time I look at the sky."

"You live with it," Laura said. "You let it make your faith bigger instead of making you crazy. God's blown your mind so your mind can grow as the previous boxes were too small. You stay humble, stay grateful, and remember that God's ways aren't our ways."

It was good counsel. Over the following months, Carl tried to follow it. He returned to flying, completed his service contract, and eventually transitioned to commercial aviation. The military years faded into memory, but that one night over the Gulf remained vivid, undiminished by time.

He never saw the lights again or anything like them. Part of him hoped he would; part of him was relieved he didn't. Once had been enough—enough to crack open his certainties, enough to introduce wonder into a life that had been too comfortable with easy answers.

Lights in the Sky

Years later, now flying commercial routes across the country, Carl would occasionally privately share his story. Not often, and not carelessly. But when the moment seemed right—at a men's retreat, in a late-night conversation with a fellow pilot, during a Bible study when the topic of angels came up—he'd tell what he witnessed.

The reactions varied. Some clearly thought he'd seen military tech and misinterpreted it. Others nodded knowingly, having had their own unexplained experiences or known others who had. A few responded with immediate hostility, warning him about demonic deception and the dangers of opening himself to the enemy's schemes.

Carl learned to discern his audience. He didn't argue with skeptics or try to convince anyone. He simply testified: "This is what I saw. This is how it affected me. Make of it what you will."

Because ultimately, that's all any witness can do—tell the truth as they experienced it and trust others to test it against Scripture, reason, and the witness of the Spirit in their own lives.

Carl Peterson is now still flying, still looking up at the same stars his father showed him in Oklahoma. His faith has matured, deepened, become less certain about details and more certain about essentials: God is real, God is vast, God still works in the world in ways that surprise us.

The lights over the Gulf remain unexplained in any official sense. The report disappeared into classified files, as Carl knew it would. But it's not disappeared from his memory or his life. It sits there as a touchstone, a reminder that reality is larger than our categories, that heaven's methods might not match our expectations, and that sometimes—just sometimes—we get to see the wheels within wheels, the chariots of fire, the lights that declare God's glory in ways that leave us breathless.

When people ask Carl if he believes in angels, he says simply: "I believe in what Scripture teaches about them. And I believe I encountered something over the Gulf that night that was beyond human technology, that radiated peace, and that left me more aware of God's presence than I'd ever been. Whether that was an angel specifically, or something else God sent, I don't claim to know. But I know it was holy. And I know I'm grateful to have seen it."

REFLECTION

Carl Peterson's encounter forces us to grapple with a question the modern church has largely avoided: What do we do with phenomena that don't fit our categories?

For centuries, Christians have spoken confidently about angels—invisible messengers who occasionally manifest to deliver God's word, protect His people, or execute His judgment. We're comfortable with the nativity angel announcing Christ's birth, or the angel rolling away the stone from Jesus' tomb. Those encounters fit neatly in our theological boxes.

But what about encounters that sound more like a Pentagon briefing than a Sunday school lesson? What about trained military pilots observing objects that violate known physics? What about radar confirmations of impossible speeds and movements? Do we dismiss these because they don't match our preconceptions of how angels should behave?

Consider Ezekiel's vision. He saw "a windstorm coming out of the north—an immense cloud with flashing lightning and surrounded by brilliant light" (Ezekiel 1:4). Within this phenomenon were creatures with four faces, wheels within wheels, rims full of eyes, moving in perfect synchronization with "the spirit of the living creatures" (Ezekiel 1:20-21). The whole vision was so overwhelming that Ezekiel fell facedown. Does metaphor make people fall facedown?

Now imagine a modern Air Force pilot reporting: "I observed a luminous object approaching from the north at high velocity. It demonstrated intelligent control, performed maneuvers impossible for known aircraft, and appeared to observe my position before departing at speeds exceeding Mach 10. The encounter left me with a profound sense of having witnessed something beyond human technology."

Are these descriptions really so different?

The Bible's angelophanies consistently include elements we'd call "paranormal" today: sudden appearances and disappearances (Judges 6:21), superhuman strength (2 Kings 19:35), ability to manipulate physical matter (Acts 12:7-10), and manifestations of light (Luke 2:9). Angels appear in fire (Exodus 3:2), in storms (2 Kings 2:11), and in visions that defy normal perception (Daniel 10:5-6).

The Magi followed a "star" that moved contrary to celestial mechanics, stopping over a specific location (Matthew 2:9-10). Whatever this was, it wasn't behaving like Jupiter or Venus. It was guided—intelligently controlled—to fulfill divine purpose.

So why do we assume that angelic activity must conform to our expectations? Why couldn't angels—beings described as having powers beyond our comprehension—manifest in ways that look technological to modern eyes?

The Hebrew word for angel, *malak*, simply means "messenger." It's a functional term, not a description of form or appearance. Angels take whatever form serves their purpose. In Genesis 18-19, they appear as ordinary men, indistinguishable until they reveal supernatural knowledge or power. (The New Testament confirms this saying some of us have entertained angels unawares. (Hebrews 13:2)) In Exodus 3, an angel appears as fire in a bush. In Ezekiel 1, they're part of a complex mechanism of wheels and living creatures that exceeds the prophet's ability to describe.

This multiplicity of forms suggests angels aren't bound to any single appearance. They manifest as needed to accomplish their purpose—which makes sense if they're spiritual beings with power over physical matter. I ask again, why would we expect them to always look like Renaissance paintings?

In fact, Renaissance angel imagery—beautiful humans with feathered wings—doesn't match biblical descriptions very well.

Biblical angels are often terrifying, so overwhelming that their first words are usually "Do not be afraid" (Luke 1:13, 30; 2:10; Matthew 28:5).

When Jacob wrestles an angel, he emerges injured, recognizing he's survived an encounter with divine power (Genesis 32:24-30). When an angel appears to Manoah and his wife, they think they're going to die (Judges 13:22).

The angels of Scripture are powerful, strange, sometimes beautiful but often overwhelming. They're messengers but also warriors, guardians but also executors of judgment. They operate according to principles we don't fully understand, with abilities that exceed our physics.

So when Carl describes seeing a luminous object that moved in impossible ways, that radiated inexplicable peace, that seemed to observe with intelligence before departing—why is our first instinct to say "That can't be an angel"? Based on what biblical standard? That it is too high tech?!

The truth is, we don't have a clear biblical standard for what angels must look like. We have descriptions of specific manifestations in specific contexts, but no systematic angelology that limits their forms. Hebrews 13:2 even suggests angels sometimes appear so ordinary we don't recognize them as angels at all.

Perhaps the real issue is our discomfort with mystery. We want angels to be explainable, categorizable, fitting into our systematic theologies. But Scripture presents them as mysterious—beings who exist primarily in the spiritual realm but can manifest physically, who possess knowledge beyond ours but serve God's purposes, who are both personal and alien to our experience.

Dr. Michael Heiser, an American biblical scholar who specialised in the divine council and spiritual realm, notes that ancient Israelites didn't see sharp distinctions between "natural" and "supernatural." For them, God's power operated through both ordinary means and extraordinary manifestations, often simultaneously. The parting of the Red Sea involved both natural wind and divine timing (Exodus

14:21). Gideon's victory over Midian involved both military strategy and angelic intervention (Judges 7).

Perhaps we need to recover this more integrated view.

What if angelic activity doesn't replace natural laws but works through and beyond them? What if God's messengers can manifest using principles we don't yet understand—principles that involve light, energy, and movement in ways that seem technological to us but are simply their nature?

This doesn't mean every UFO is an angel. It means we shouldn't automatically dismiss the possibility, especially when an encounter bears the marks of divine activity: many occurring in response to prayer, producing long lasting peace rather than terror (but many Biblical prophets were terrified so us being afraid *at the time* is not the test of whether something is demonic), leading toward God rather than away from Him. (But recalling we can all fall, so I reiterate, "fruit" is not the ultimate test. Time and again, I've heard Christian witnesses of UFOs tell me they "fell" because of *others'* reactions afterwards, so after becoming isolated from their churches because their churches did not have big enough theological constructs to contain their experiences. They were thus led instead down New Age rabbit holes.).

Carl's encounter bears the plausible marks of divine activity. He was on routine patrol—not seeking anything unusual. The object appeared, demonstrated abilities beyond human technology, but radiated peace rather than threat. Carl felt no compulsion to worship it or seek it out again. Instead, he found himself drawn deeper into Scripture, prayer, and wonder at God's creativity.

The test Scripture provides for spiritual discernment isn't

"Does this match my expectations?" but "Does this acknowledge the Lordship of Jesus Christ and produce good fruit?" (1 John 4:2-3; Matthew 7:16-20). By those measures, Carl's encounter passes.

Some will argue this opens dangerous doors—that if we allow UFOs might be angels, we'll end up accepting all sorts of New Age deception. That's a valid concern. Satan can masquerade as an angel of light (2 Corinthians 11:14), and not everything supernatural is godly.

But the solution isn't to deny all extraordinary experience. It's to apply biblical tests rigorously.

Carl never claimed special revelation. He never started a ministry based on his sighting. He never sought attention or profit. He simply integrated the experience into his existing faith, allowing it to deepen his wonder at God's creativity while maintaining his commitment to Scripture as his authority.

That's how encounters with the holy should function—not replacing biblical truth but enriching our appreciation of how vast and creative God is in accomplishing His purposes.

The "chariots of God" that Elisha's servant saw surrounding the prophet (2 Kings 6:17) weren't metaphorical. They were real enough to provide actual protection. Yet they were visible only when spiritual eyes were opened. What else might be present that we don't yet have eyes to see?

C.S. Lewis wrote: "I believe in Christianity as I believe that the sun has risen: not only because I see it, but because by it I see everything else." Perhaps encounters like Carl's serve a similar purpose—not as objects of faith themselves, but as events that help us see our faith more clearly, that remind us God's world is larger than our maps of it.

The lights over the Gulf remain unexplained in any official sense—to us, at least. (Perhaps in the age of Disclosure more will come out.) But for Carl Peterson, they became a window into deeper reality—a glimpse of the wheels within wheels, the chariots of fire, the ways God's glory manifests in creation. Not to replace Scripture or tradition, but to confirm that the God of the Bible still works wonders, still sends His messengers, still declares His glory through the heavens.

And perhaps that's enough: not complete understanding, but confirmed wonder. Not all questions answered, but faith expanded. Not certainty about mechanisms, but assurance that we serve a God whose ways exceed our categories and whose messengers might appear in forms stranger and more wonderful than we ever imagined.

TESTIMONY 2
ANGELS IN THE CORNFIELD

HENRY CALDWELL had worked the same Iowa farmland for forty-three years. He knew every rise and hollow, every shift of wind, every pattern the corn made as it ripened under the summer sun. The land didn't surprise him anymore—or so he thought.

The Caldwell family had farmed this section of Iowa since 1887, when Henry's great-grandfather claimed the homestead from prairie that stretched unbroken to the horizon. Each generation added something: a barn, a second silo, irrigation systems that pulled water from the deep aquifer beneath the black soil.

The land had been generous to them, mostly. There had been lean years—the Depression, the farm crisis of the '80s—but the Caldwells survived when others didn't, through a combination of hard work, careful stewardship, and what Henry's grandfather called "the Lord's favor."

Henry's grandfather was a man of few words but deep faith. He'd sit on the porch in the evenings, Bible in his lap, watching the sunset paint the western sky in shades of gold and crimson.

"God made this land," he'd say. "Loaned it to us for a season. Our job is to tend it well and give thanks." He taught young Henry and his older sister Martha to pray before planting, to thank God at harvest, to see farming not just as business but as partnership with the Creator.

That theology shaped Henry's approach to the land. He wasn't mystical by nature—he was practical, methodical, the kind of farmer who studied soil reports and attended agricultural extension seminars. But underneath the pragmatism ran a quiet awareness that something more than chemistry and climatology governed the land's fruitfulness. He prayed over his fields each spring, asking blessing on the seed. He tithed from his harvest, even in lean years. And he maintained a posture of gratitude that kept him humble even in prosperous times.

It was late August, that brief window when the corn reached full height and the harvest loomed but hadn't yet begun. The evening air hung thick with moisture, carrying the sweet earthiness of corn in full tassel. Henry walked the fence line as he did most nights, checking for breaks, listening to the familiar sounds: crickets building their chorus, distant cattle lowing, the soft whisper of corn leaves brushing together in the breeze.

The ritual was meditative, almost sacramental. These evening walks let Henry decompress from the day's work, assess the fields with fresh eyes, and spend time in prayer. He'd thank God for the day, lift up concerns, and often just walk in silence, attuned to the land and the sky and the subtle presence he'd learned to recognize in both.

The sun had set perhaps thirty minutes earlier, leaving that peculiar twilight where details blur but darkness hasn't yet claimed the land. Henry was about to turn back toward the house when he noticed the light.

At first, he assumed it was his neighbor's truck, maybe checking cattle in the back forty. But the glow was wrong—

too steady, too golden, and positioned oddly between rows of corn about a hundred yards out. As he watched, the light pulsed gently, like a heartbeat made visible.

Henry's practical mind ran through possibilities: lightning bug swarm (wrong color, wrong season), methane from the creek bed (wrong behavior), someone playing with drones (wrong era—this was 1985, before consumer drones existed).

The light wasn't moving randomly. It hovered with apparent purpose, occasionally drifting laterally but maintaining consistent altitude just above the corn tassels.

He should have been afraid. Decades of horror movies and news reports had conditioned Americans to fear strange lights. But Henry felt no fear—only curiosity and a growing sense of... rightness. As if this was meant to happen, as if he was meant to witness it.

He moved forward, feet finding the worn path between rows almost automatically. The corn was over seven feet tall here, creating a natural corridor. As Henry approached, he could hear nothing but his own breathing and the soft crunch of his boots on dry earth. Even the crickets had gone silent—not ominously, but expectantly, like the pause before a symphony begins.

Then he saw them.

Not one light, but three, arranged in a loose triangle, hovering approximately twelve feet above the ground. They pulsed in sequence—left, center, right, left—creating a rhythm that felt almost conversational, like beings communicating in a language of light. The golden glow illuminated the corn below, casting long shadows that swayed in the evening breeze, creating patterns of light and dark that seemed too beautiful to be random.

Henry stopped about thirty feet away, heart pounding but not from fear. He felt... observed. Not threatened, but acknowledged. Like standing before someone who knows you completely yet holds no judgment. Like being in the presence of the holy.

"Hello?" His voice was cracked, uncertain. He felt foolish speaking to lights, yet not speaking felt wrong too. Something about their behavior suggested awareness, even intelligence.

The lights pulsed faster, maintaining their pattern but with increased intensity. Henry had the strangest impression of greeting, though nothing was spoken. No words formed in his mind. Just a sense of recognition, of being seen and known.

He stood transfixed, aware that he should probably run, tell someone, grab a camera—but unable to move. His body remained rooted while his mind struggled to process what his eyes reported. The lights weren't solid objects. They seemed to be made of light itself, semi-transparent, with an internal structure he couldn't quite focus on. When he tried to look directly at the center of one light, his eyes would slide away as if unable to fix on it, yet he could see it perfectly in his peripheral vision.

How long he stood there, he couldn't later say. Time felt suspended, elastic. The lights continued their pulsing dance, occasionally adjusting their formation slightly—the triangle would widen, then tighten, then shift to form a straight line before returning to triangle formation. The movements were too precise to be random, too graceful to be mechanical.

They felt intentional, purposeful, almost... playful.

Then, gradually, a thought formed in Henry's mind that didn't appear to come from his own thinking. Not words exactly, but a clear impression that translated into language: *You are known. Your work matters. The land is blessed.*

Henry's throat tightened. He'd prayed dozens of times over the years—especially during tough seasons when drought threatened or prices fell. *Lord, see my work. Let it matter. Bless this land.* Had these lights somehow heard those prayers? Were they an answer?

The lights began rising slowly, maintaining their formation. As they ascended, Henry noticed more details he'd somehow missed before: subtle color variations in the golden glow, hints of green and blue at the edges; the way air seemed to shimmer around them without heat; the absolute silence of their movement, not even the whisper of displaced air.

They rose perhaps two hundred feet, hovered briefly at that height, then shot straight up with impossible acceleration, vanishing into the darkening sky. The speed was so great Henry couldn't track the movement—they were there, then gone, leaving only afterimages burned into his vision.

The evening sounds rushed back immediately: crickets resuming mid-song, distant cattle calling, corn rustling in a breeze he suddenly felt again on his face. Everything ordinary except Henry's thundering heart and the unmistakable conviction that he'd just witnessed something extraordinary.

He walked home slowly, mind reeling. His sister, Martha,

who'd been living with him since his wife passed, took one look at his face and poured coffee without asking.

"Did you see it?" he asked her breathlessly.

She shook her head. "See what?"

Henry told her everything, words tumbling out, expecting her to suggest exhaustion or heat stroke or some rational explanation that would let them both dismiss what he'd seen.

Instead, she reached across the table and squeezed his hand. "Them fields have been blessed before," she said quietly. "Our grandfather saw lights over the corn the year of the great drought—1934. Every farm around us failed that summer. Ours didn't. Lost some of the harvest, yes, but enough came through to keep us going. He always said angels protected it."

Henry blinked. "He told you that?"

"Yeah. When I was a kid. I guess you must have been about two at the time. I mostly forgot it—but the way you're describing it…" Martha's eyes grew distant. "He said they looked like lamps floating in the air, moving with purpose. He thought they were watching over the land."

"You never mentioned this before."

Martha shrugged. "You were too young. And honestly, as I got older, I half thought it was just a family story that got embellished over time. But now…" She looked at Henry steadily. "What do you think was out there tonight?"

"I can't say," Henry admitted. "I know what it looked like —some kind of craft, or beings, or... I don't know. But it didn't feel threatening. It felt..." He struggled for words. "It felt like being in church. That moment of holy awe during worship when everything goes quiet and you're aware that something holy is happening even if you can't explain what. It was like that, I guess."

Martha nodded slowly. "Maybe that's answer enough. Maybe we're not meant to explain everything, just recognize when we're in the presence of God's work."

* * *

The next morning, Henry half expected to find his experience fading like a dream, details fuzzing at the edges. Instead, the memory remained crystalline. He walked to the spot where he'd stood the night before, half-expecting burn marks or flattened corn—something physical to prove it had been real.

The corn was untouched. No evidence remained. But as Henry stood between the rows, he noticed something he'd overlooked in forty-three years of farming: the way morning sunlight caught the silk, creating golden halos around each ear. The way dew sparkled on leaves like scattered jewels. The extraordinary beauty of ordinary things.

He knelt, touched the soil, and prayed: *Thank you. Whatever that was, thank you for letting me see it. Help me be faithful to what you've entrusted to me.*

Rising, he surveyed the fields stretching to the horizon. The same land he'd walked countless times, yet somehow transformed by the previous night's encounter. He didn't understand what he'd witnessed. But he felt profoundly grateful to have witnessed it.

He told no one outside his sister for years. In their farming community, practicality ruled. Men discussed soil pH and commodity prices, weather patterns and market futures, not mystical encounters. Henry had no desire to become the local eccentric or, worse, be dismissed as either a liar or unstable.

But the experience changed him in subtle ways. He found himself praying more—not formal prayers recited by rote, but conversations with God while working. Thanking Him for rain. Asking guidance about planting decisions. Acknowledging that the land, ultimately, wasn't his but held in trust for something larger.

The harvests that followed were unremarkable by conventional standards—good years and lean years like any farmer experiences. No miraculous abundance that would make national news. Yet Henry noticed a pattern: every time disaster threatened (early frost, hail storm, pest infestation), something intervened. A wind shift at the critical moment. An unexpected temperature change.

Natural events, yes, but timed so precisely that Henry couldn't dismiss them as mere luck.

The early frost of 1989 should have devastated the corn. Weather services had predicted temperatures dropping to 28 degrees—low enough to kill the crop that was still three weeks from maturity. Henry spent the evening preparing for loss, mentally calculating whether the insurance would cover costs. He went to bed heavy-hearted, praying for mercy but expecting the worst.

Around 3 AM, he woke to the sound of wind—unusual for that time of night in late September. He looked out the bedroom window and saw clouds rolling in from the southwest, thick and low. By morning, the temperature had stayed above freezing. The clouds dissipated by noon, and the corn continued maturing. Two weeks later, it was safely harvested.

The neighboring farms, three miles north where the clouds hadn't reached, lost most of their crop to frost.

In 1992, a hailstorm swept through the county, devastating farms in a line that cut straight through Caldwell land. Yet Henry's fields sustained only minor damage—as if the storm had parted around them.

These events weren't supernatural in the obvious sense. They were natural weather phenomena. But their timing, their precise targeting, felt like more than coincidence. Henry simply gave quiet thanks and continued his work, aware that something was watching over the land in ways he couldn't explain but deeply appreciated.

But something far more profound had happened than a simple reminder that God was providing for him materially. The deep, aching grief over his wife's death from breast cancer—a weight he had carried for more than two years—had suddenly lifted. In its place settled a quiet, steady peace and a certainty (not merely a belief) that he would see her again. It was as if the lights had taken the sorrow with them.

Five years after the lights, Henry told his story to his pastor during a hospital visit—Henry was recovering from minor surgery, and the pastor had stopped by with communion. Propped up in the hospital bed, feeling vulnerable and reflective, Henry found the words spilling out.

Pastor Martinez a young man fresh from seminary, listened politely but his expression revealed skepticism. When Henry finished, the pastor offered a gentle smile:

"God works in mysterious ways. Perhaps it was a vision, a dream given to strengthen your faith during hard times."

"It weren't no dream," Henry said firmly. "I was wide awake. Walking the fence line like I do every evening. What I saw was as real as you sitting in that chair."

Pastor Martinez shifted uncomfortably. "I'm not questioning your sincerity, Henry. But we need to be careful about attributing every unusual sight to divine activity. There could be natural explanations—atmospheric conditions, aircraft—"

"At ground level? Moving between corn rows? Silent?" Henry shook his head. "I know what aircraft look like. I know what weather phenomena look like. This was neither."

The pastor left shortly after, clearly uncomfortable with the conversation. Henry never brought it up again at church, though he noticed the pastor treating him with a certain cautiousness afterward—polite but distant, as if Henry had revealed himself to be less stable than previously thought.

The rejection — and the appraisal — stung, but it also clarified something for Henry. His church, he realized, had no category for what he'd experienced. They'd boxed angels into neat theological concepts: spiritual beings who occasionally appeared as humans in biblical times, but nothing more. The idea that divine messengers might manifest as lights, might still be active, might appear to an ordinary farmer in Iowa—that didn't fit their boxes.

Instead of seeking a new church, Henry stopped trying to make it fit. He held the experience privately, a treasure known only to him and Martha —and then later, me —and lived the remainder of his years as faithful as he knew how.

Lights in the Sky

The lights didn't return, but he often felt their presence—a sense of being watched over, protected, acknowledged in his daily work.

***

Years passed. In time, Henry's family took over the farm —first his son Tom, then eventually Tom's children. The family business continued across generations, as it had for over a century. Henry's testimony (and his grandfather's) had been written down so future generations of the Caldwells could know of God's provision long after his death.

I've checked in with them over the years and several family members, despite a couple of them not 'really' believing in God, report their own sightings—not the same detailed encounter Henry had experienced, but brief glimpses: golden lights hovering over the fields at dusk, visible for a few seconds before vanishing. One sighting notably was from a witness not even familiar with Henry's story as she'd just started dating Henry's grandson.

The farm meanwhile has prospered quietly. No miracles by modern standards, just consistent harvests and a strange pattern of narrow escapes from agricultural disasters that would have devastated less fortunate neighbors. It appears that God is still answering the old man's prayers long after his passing.

Were these interventions? Divine protection? Or just good management and fortunate timing? The family debated it occasionally, usually around holiday tables when multiple generations gathered. But they all agreed on one thing: something special watched over the land. Whether you called it angels, God's blessing, or just luck, the pattern was undeniable.

When I'd visited Henry just before his passing, he'd walked me along that same fence line despite his slow pace and reliance on a cane. The land looked ordinary enough: Iowa farmland like thousands of other properties, corn standing tall in late summer, a few clouds drifting lazily across the blue sky. But as we stood where he'd first seen the lights decades ago, Henry pointed skyward with a gnarled finger.

"Angels or something else, I can't say for certain, Joe," he told me. "But I know they weren't hostile. I know they acknowledged me. And I know that for one night, I weren't just a farmer tending corn—I was part of something vast and beautiful."

He paused, scanning the darkening horizon as sunset approached. "The land is His. The heavens are His. If He wants to send angels that look like lights in the sky... he sure well can! Who's anyone to disagree with God!"

I couldn't argue with that logic. Standing there in the gathering dusk, surrounded by corn and cricket-song, I understood why he'd never needed complete explanation. Some encounters are meant to be witnessed and treasured, not dissected and explained.

A month after my visit, Henry passed away quietly in his sleep. At the funeral, two of his grandchildren separately told me they'd seen the lights the night he died—golden pulses hovering over the farmhouse around midnight then ascending straight up until they vanished into the stars.

Coincidence? Mass hallucination? Or perhaps angels

escorting a faithful servant home? (I know of other witnesses who saw UFOs just after a loved one's passing).

I don't claim to know. But I believe Henry's testimony, and I believe the land he tended remains somehow marked by what he witnessed. The Caldwell farm continues to prosper. Crop yields consistently exceed county averages by small but steady margins. The soil tests richer than comparable land nearby. And on clear summer nights, family members occasionally report seeing lights—brief flashes of gold above the corn, there and gone before cameras can capture them. One time, Amelia, one of his granddaughters, stayed out in the fields with a video camera, only for the video and also her phone to malfunction just at the point the lights appeared.

The farm has become a quiet witness to something beyond agricultural science, something the Caldwells speak of carefully but hold deeply: the land is watched over. By angels, by God's providence, by forces that operate in whispers rather than shouts. The lights Henry saw were just one visible manifestation of a care that operates continuously, mostly unseen, protecting and blessing those faithful to Him.

And on summer nights, if you stand at that fence line and watch carefully, you might just see what Henry saw: lights that dance above the corn with purpose and grace, reminders that creation is wider and wilder and more wonderful than our tidy categories allow. Just don't expect to be able to catch it on video.

Joe Lighthall

REFLECTION: Servants in Unexpected Forms

Henry Caldwell's encounter challenges our assumptions about where and how divine messengers appear. We expect angels in cathedrals, perhaps, or at dramatic moments of crisis. We don't expect them hovering over Iowa cornfields on ordinary Tuesday evenings.

Yet Scripture is full of angels appearing in mundane contexts to ordinary people: Abraham entertaining strangers who turn out to be angels (Hebrews 13:2, referencing Genesis 18), Gideon meeting an angel while threshing wheat (Judges 6:11-12), shepherds receiving the nativity announcement while watching flocks (Luke 2:8-14). God's messengers show up not where we think they should, but where God chooses to send them.

The rural context matters. Farming communities are often dismissed as backward, unsophisticated, places where "real" spirituality doesn't happen. The assumption runs: if God wants to manifest dramatically, He'll do it in Jerusalem, Rome, or at minimum a major metropolitan area. But Scripture contradicts this. God reveals Himself repeatedly in rural settings: to shepherds, farmers, fishermen. The incarnation itself occurred in a backwater town that prompted Nathanael's dismissive "Can anything good come from Nazareth?" (John 1:46).

Perhaps farmland—places where humans actively partner with creation's rhythms, depending on rain and sun and soil—are exactly where divine manifestation makes sense. Henry wasn't passive. He was a steward, tending land entrusted to him, working in cooperation with natural processes he understood but couldn't control. That posture of active dependence mirrors our relationship with God: we work faithfully while acknowledging ultimate outcomes rest beyond our power.

The description Henry gave—lights arranged in formation, hovering with apparent intelligence, creating a sense of presence and peace—echoes biblical accounts more than it might first appear. When angels appear in Scripture, light is consistently part of the manifestation: "An angel of the Lord appeared to them, and the glory of the Lord shone around them" (Luke 2:9). The angel at Jesus' tomb had "an appearance like lightning" (Matthew 28:3). Even the descriptions of heavenly beings in Revelation emphasize brilliance and radiance (Revelation 10:1).

But what about the technology-like aspects—the formation, the coordinated movement, the seemingly mechanical precision? Here's where Ezekiel becomes crucial. His vision of the cherubim includes details that sound strikingly like advanced machinery: wheels intersecting wheels, movements in perfect coordination, "fire moving back and forth" between the creatures, and motion that goes "wherever the spirit would go" without turning (Ezekiel 1:15-21).

Were these literal mechanical devices? Or was Ezekiel—a man from the ancient world—describing spiritual realities in the only technological language he knew? Perhaps the real question is: why would we expect angels to appear primitive simply because they're spiritual beings?

The prophet describes the wheels as having "rims...full of

eyes all around" (Ezekiel 1:18). This detail suggests awareness, intelligence, perhaps even multiple perspectives or dimensions of perception. The entire structure moved in perfect coordination, "wherever the spirit would go." This isn't random or chaotic—it's organized, purposeful, almost machine-like in its precision.

Now imagine trying to describe such a vision to an agrarian society that had no concept of flight beyond birds, no machinery beyond simple tools and wheels. Ezekiel does remarkably well with the language he has: wheels, fire, creatures with multiple faces, coordinated movement. But he repeatedly uses qualifiers—"like," "as if," "the appearance of"—because he's reaching the limits of vocabulary.

What if Henry saw something similar? Not identical, perhaps, but the same class of manifestation—spiritual beings made visible, taking forms that involve light, geometry, coordinated movement? What if his description of "wheels within wheels" wasn't metaphorical borrowing from Ezekiel but independent observation of the same phenomenon?

C.S. Lewis explored this in his Space Trilogy, particularly *Perelandra* and *That Hideous Strength*. In *That Hideous Strength*, Lewis describes the "eldila"—spiritual beings who can manipulate matter and energy, who move through space in ways that seem technological to observers but are simply their nature. When characters encounter them, the experience is both technological (lights, energy, precise movements) and numinous (overwhelming presence, sense of the holy).

Lewis was drawing on classical angelology for his works

of fiction, which understood angels as having power over physical creation. Thomas Aquinas wrote extensively about angelic abilities: they can move instantaneously, manipulate matter, appear in bodies temporarily assumed for specific purposes. They're not bound by our physics but can work within it when necessary.

If angels possess such abilities—and Scripture consistently portrays them as powerful, capable of dramatic physical interventions—why wouldn't their manifestations sometimes look technological? Why would we expect them to always appear in first-century Palestinian human form?

Henry's encounter left him blessed, not traumatized. It deepened his faith rather than leading him into obsession. The message—implicit but clear—was one of care, acknowledgment, and assurance. And of the knowledge he would see his wife again. He was healed instantaneously of his gnawing grief. These are consistent marks of genuinely holy encounters throughout Scripture.

Contrast this with accounts that bear different fruit. When encounters produce fear without peace (that is: peace in the long run), demand worship of the phenomenon itself, lead to obsession rather than integration, or move people away from Scripture and Christian community—those are warning signs. Scripture teaches us to test spirits (1 John 4:1-3), and fruit is a primary test.

By that measure, Henry's experience bears good fruit: increased faith, sustained gratitude, quiet service, integration into existing biblical faith rather than replacement of it. He didn't start a UFO cult. He didn't claim special revelation beyond Scripture. He didn't seek profit or attention. He simply allowed the encounter to deepen his existing relationship with God, making him more aware of divine presence in daily work.

Some will object that we shouldn't confuse UFO phenomena with angels. Fair enough—I'm not suggesting all sightings are angelic. I will say once again that many likely have natural explanations we don't yet understand. Some may be human technology, classified or experimental. And Scripture warns that Satan himself masquerades as an angel of light (2 Corinthians 11:14), so discernment remains essential.

But I am suggesting we shouldn't automatically dismiss encounters like Henry's simply because they don't match our preconceptions. Angels in the Bible do strange things: they feed people with supernatural food (1 Kings 19:5-6), roll away multi-ton stones (Matthew 28:2), strike entire armies dead overnight (2 Kings 19:35), and appear in forms that terrify until they announce "Do not be afraid."

If God created the universe—all the galaxies, all the dimensions we barely understand, all the physical laws we're still discovering—why would we expect His messengers to be simple? Why couldn't beings exist who operate according to principles that look like advanced technology to us but are simply their nature?

The crucial question isn't "Was that a UFO or an angel?" but rather "Was that —whatever if was—a messenger from God?"

Henry's cornfield visitors—whatever their nature—served the purposes of heaven: assuring a faithful man that his labor mattered, that he was seen and valued, that the created world operates under divine care. They healed an old man's aching heart and age him assurance of the hereafter. The subsequent pattern of protection over the land, while not miraculous in obvious ways, suggests ongoing divine attention.

Perhaps we need to expand our categories. Not every light in the sky is an angel, certainly. But not every angelic encounter will match our Renaissance paintings either. God is creative. His messengers are diverse. And the chariots of God—whatever form they take—are still at work in the world, often in the most unexpected places.

A cornfield in Iowa. A shepherd's field outside Bethlehem. A threshing floor in Ophrah. God's pattern remains consistent: appearing to ordinary people in ordinary places, speaking messages that combine the profound and the practical, leaving behind not confusion but wonder.

Henry Caldwell spent the rest of his life as a better farmer, a better Christian, and a better man because of what he witnessed. If that's not the fruit of a holy encounter, what is?

The land continues to prosper quietly. The family continues faithful stewardship. And occasionally, when the light is right and the heart is attentive, golden pulses appear above the corn—brief, undeniable, gone before skepticism can dismiss them and video can catch them. Reminders that we are not alone, that creation is watched over, that the God of Ezekiel's wheels still sends His messengers to encourage those who labor faithfully in His fields.

TESTIMONY 3
THE DESERT ENCOUNTER

AHIGA TSOSIE had been walking the desert alone for three hours when night fell completely. The sun had slipped behind the mesas, leaving that brief purple twilight before darkness claimed the land. He was seventeen miles from the nearest road, following a path his grandfather had shown him years ago—one of the old Navajo trails that wound between juniper and sage.

He'd come seeking silence. At twenty-three, Ahiga worked in Phoenix, lived in a cramped apartment, spent his days amid noise and traffic and the constant churn of urban life. The desert was his reset button, the place where he could hear himself think and, more importantly, hear God.

Ahiga's grandfather had taught him to pray this way—not with many words, but with presence.

"Go to the quiet places," the old man would say. "God speaks in whispers. You can't hear whispers in the city." So Ahiga made these pilgrimage walks several times a year, taking vacation days to drive out to the reservation, park his truck at a trailhead, and walk into the vast emptiness that had shaped his people for centuries.

The Navajo Nation—Dinétah, "among the people"—sprawled across portions of Arizona, New Mexico, and Utah, encompassing deserts, mesas, and canyons that held both beauty and danger. The land demanded respect. People died here regularly: hikers underestimating distances, tourists ignoring weather warnings, occasional foolish souls who wandered off marked trails without water or preparation.

But Ahiga knew this land. His grandfather had taught him to read it: how to find water by watching birds, how to navigate by stars and landmarks, how to recognize the subtle signs of weather changes hours before they arrived. More importantly, his grandfather had taught him to see the land as sacred—not just beautiful or useful, but holy, a place where the physical and spiritual intertwined.

"Our ancestors knew the world was alive," his grandfather had told him. "The stones, the wind, the rain—all had spirit. When the missionaries came, they said these were false gods. But I think maybe we were seeing the same truth from different angles. The Bible talks about creation groaning, waiting for redemption. The land has spirit because God made it that way. We just gave it different names."

Ahiga had grown up navigating this tension—Navajo tradition and Christian faith, his grandfather's wisdom and his pastor's teaching. Some elders said you had to choose one or the other. But Ahiga's grandfather had integrated both: attending church on Sunday, performing traditional blessings for family, seeing no contradiction.

"Jesus walked on this earth," he'd say. "He touched rocks and sand and water. He blessed creation. Why should it surprise us that creation responds to blessing, that it carries echoes of the holy?"

The stars emerged gradually as Ahiga walked, then suddenly blazed into full brilliance. The Milky Way sprawled overhead like a river of light, so dense and bright it cast faint shadows. Ahiga spread his sleeping bag on a flat rock outcropping and sat watching the sky, praying in the way his grandfather had taught him—wordless attention, simply being present to whatever God might say.

The desert night carried its own sounds: distant yips of coyotes, the occasional rustle of small creatures in the brush, the whisper of wind across stone. But underneath these sounds lay a deeper silence—not absence of noise but presence of stillness, the kind that presses against you and invites you inward.

Ahiga sat in that stillness for perhaps an hour, thoughts gradually quieting, breath matching the rhythm of the night. He prayed for guidance—he was at a crossroads, considering whether to leave his job in Phoenix, whether to move back to the reservation, whether to pursue teaching or stay in construction. Questions without easy answers.

Then the lights appeared.

Three of them at first, rising over a distant ridge perhaps half a mile away. They moved too slowly to be meteors, too fast and fluid to be aircraft. As Ahiga watched, they performed a series of movements that defied everything he knew about flight: sudden stops mid-air, right-angle turns without slowing, accelerations that should have created sonic booms but remained utterly silent.

His first thought was military test flights. Plenty of restricted airspace in this part of Arizona—the Barry M. Goldwater Range covered vast stretches of desert where the military tested everything from missiles to experimental aircraft. But these movements were wrong—too abrupt, too varied, too... playful. The lights seemed to be dancing, weaving patterns against the stars like fireflies, but on a massive scale and with impossible precision.

More lights appeared. Five. Seven. A dozen. They formed geometric patterns—triangles, lines, circles—then dissolved and reformed in new configurations. No sound reached him. No engine roar, no helicopter thump, no jet whine. Just silent movement and that golden-white glow that seemed to emanate from within rather than reflecting external sources.

Ahiga felt no fear. Instead, despite the exhilaration, an overwhelming peace settled over him, the same sensation he'd felt during his baptism years ago—the sense of being held, protected, known. Not the absence of self, but the presence of something larger that contained and confirmed his self. He stood slowly, arms at his sides, watching the impossible display.

Then a thought formed in his mind, clear as if spoken aloud: *Walk*.

It wasn't his own thought. The certainty was too complete, the direction too specific. When you think your own thoughts, there's always a slight hesitation, a sense of your mind forming ideas. This thought appeared whole, immediate, external.

Ahiga didn't decide to walk—he was told to walk, and his body responded before his conscious mind could question.

He grabbed his pack and started walking, not back toward the truck but deeper into the desert, following the lights that now moved ahead of him. They maintained distance—perhaps a hundred yards ahead—pulsing gently like beacons, always visible but never close enough to touch.

The rational part of his mind protested: This is dangerous. You're leaving the trail. You could get lost, break an ankle, die out here. But a deeper knowing overrode those fears. The lights were guiding him. He was meant to follow.

He walked for what might have been thirty minutes or three hours—time felt strange, elastic, like dream time where minutes stretch into hours or compress into seconds. The lights stayed ahead, pulsing gently, occasionally adjusting their position but always leading in the same general direction: northeast, toward an area Ahiga had never explored.

The landscape shifted subtly as he walked. The ground became more uneven, rocks more frequent. He climbed gentle rises and descended into shallow washes, following the lights' path with trust he couldn't rationally justify. Once, he stumbled on loose stone and nearly fell, but caught himself at the last moment, steadied by adrenaline and the continued presence of the lights ahead.

Then, without warning, the lights stopped. They hovered in place, pulsing more urgently now—faster, brighter, with an intensity that communicated alarm. Ahiga slowed, suddenly wary. The ground ahead looked flat, unremarkable in the faint starlight. But the lights' behavior had changed dramatically, shifting from gentle guidance to urgent warning.

He approached cautiously, and then he saw it: the canyon.

In daylight, he might have spotted it from a distance—a jagged crack in the earth, shadows marking its depth. But in darkness, walking across this featureless stretch with only starlight to see by, he would have walked straight over the edge. The canyon wasn't dramatic—no Grand Canyon chasm, just a sixty-foot drop onto rocks and scrub brush. But sixty feet was more than enough. He would have died before morning, either from the fall itself or from injuries that left him unable to move, unable to call for help, bleeding out in the dark while coyotes circled.

Eli's legs buckled and he sat heavily on the ground, three feet from the edge, staring at the void he'd almost walked into. His hands trembled. His breath came in short gasps. The reality of what had nearly happened crashed over him in waves: one more step, maybe two, and he'd have plunged into darkness. No one knew exactly where he was. His truck sat more than seventeen miles away on the other side of a landscape he'd just been led through in darkness. Even if someone came looking, they'd never find him in time.

The lights hovered at the canyon's edge for perhaps thirty seconds, pulsing steadily. Then they rose slowly, formed a final pattern—a circle that rotated once, twice, three times—and shot straight up with impossible speed. One moment they were there, the next gone, vanishing into the star-field as if they'd never existed.

Ahiga sat until dawn, too shaken to sleep, too aware of his near-death to move. If the lights hadn't warned him, he would have been another statistic: hiker falls in desert, body found days later by searchers who'd wonder why he'd been so far off trail.

But the lights had warned him. And he was alive.

***

As the sun rose, painting the desert in shades of copper and gold, he traced his path back from where he'd been the previous night, wondering why the lights had led him this way only then to save him at the precipice. Was it a metaphor, he wondered. Or something else?

When he arrived back to where he would have slept but for the lights guiding him away, it soon became obvious. There were fresh tire marks and spent bullet cases nearby: sign of some kind of criminal activity that he would have been an inadvertent witness to had he still been there. *This* is what the lights were up to.

***

Ahiga told no one for months. The experience felt too sacred, too strange. How do you explain lights that guide you like shepherds? How do you describe a voice that wasn't audible but was unmistakably real, unmistakably external to yourself?

He returned to Phoenix, to his job, to the routines of normal life. But the encounter wouldn't leave him. It pressed on his thoughts during work meetings, surfaced in his dreams, demanded acknowledgment. The desert had given him something—or something in the desert had given him something—and he couldn't simply file it away as unusual experience and move on.

Finally, three months after the night on the canyon edge, he drove to the small Native American church his grandfather had attended—a modest building on the reservation that served the scattered Christian Navajo community. The pastor was a weathered Diné man in his sixties who'd spent decades navigating the same tensions Ahiga experienced: honoring traditional wisdom while following Christ, seeing God's work in both Scripture and creation.

Ahiga found him in the church office, working on Sunday's sermon. The pastor looked up, smiled, gestured to a worn chair.

"Ahiga Tsosie. Haven't seen you in months. Sit."

Ahiga sat. For a moment, he couldn't find words. Then they tumbled out—the whole story, from his walk into the desert to the lights to the voice to the canyon edge. He told it chronologically, simply, without embellishment or interpretation, just reporting what had happened.

The pastor listened without interruption, his weathered face unreadable. When Ahiga finished, he was silent for a long moment, fingers steepled, eyes distant.

"My grandfather told me a story," his pastor said finally. "During the Long Walk, when our people were forced from our land by the soldiers, his father saw lights in the sky. He said they led him to water when the soldiers wouldn't let them stop to drink. He believed they were the Holy People, taking care of those who still prayed."

"You think they were angels?" Ahiga asked.

His pastor smiled slightly. "Does it matter what we call them? You prayed for guidance. You were guided. You could have died. You didn't. Whether you call them angels or Holy People or something else, they served the Creator's purpose —keeping His child alive."

The affirmation felt like permission Ahiga hadn't known he needed. He'd been carrying the experience in isolation, unsure whether to trust it, afraid it might be delusion or dangerous spiritual territory. But his pastor treated it matter-of-factly, as if unusual encounters with the divine were simply part of the landscape for those who walked in faith.

"What do I do with this?" Ahiga asked. "How do I understand it?"

"You don't," the pastor said simply. "Not completely. Moses saw a burning bush and never fully understood how fire could burn without consuming. Understanding isn't always the goal. Sometimes the goal is simply to say 'yes' when God speaks, to follow when He leads, and to give thanks when He saves as He undoubtedly did you."

He paused, then added: "But you should know—this isn't as unusual as you think. Many of our people have seen lights, especially those who go into the desert to pray. Some see them as Holy People from traditional stories. Some see them as angels from the Bible. Maybe they're both. Maybe the Holy People and angels are different names for the same servants of the Creator."

This perspective shifted something in Ahiga. He'd been thinking in either/or terms—either these were angels (Christian explanation) or they were something from traditional Navajo spirituality (ancestral explanation). But what if they were neither and both? What if the same divine reality had been appearing to his people for generations, and different cultural frameworks simply named it differently?

The conversation with his pastor opened doors. Ahiga began researching carefully, not conspiracy websites but historical accounts, anthropological records, documented testimonies. What he found surprised him as he did not

Lights in the Sky

realise it went beyond his culture: across cultures and centuries, lights in the sky appeared to people during spiritual activities—prayer, vision quests, sacred ceremonies—and frequently provided guidance, protection, or warning.

The biblical accounts stood out. The pillar of cloud and fire that guided Israel through the wilderness (Exodus 13:21-22) moved with obvious intelligence, stopped when the people needed to camp, resumed when it was time to travel. Not random, not natural, but purposeful.

Elijah's transportation to heaven involved "chariots of fire and horses of fire" and a whirlwind (2 Kings 2:11). Elisha saw it clearly enough to describe specifics. This wasn't metaphor or vision—something dramatic and visible occurred.

The star that guided the Magi (Matthew 2:9-10) didn't follow normal celestial mechanics. Stars don't stop over specific buildings. They don't move independently of their orbital paths. Whatever the Magi followed, it moved with intelligence and purpose.

Even Jesus' ascension involved unusual phenomena: "a cloud hid him from their sight" (Acts 1:9). Not weather—a cloud, singular, that obscured the disciples' vision at the precise moment of ascension.

What if, Ahiga wondered, the ancients were describing real phenomena using the language they had? What if angels don't always appear as winged humans but sometimes manifest as lights, as fire, as clouds—as whatever form serves God's purpose?

"This was the appearance of the likeness of the glory of the Lord," Ezekiel concluded (1:28). Not "This was a spaceship" or "These were angels" but simply: *this was glory made visible, and I lack adequate words to describe it.*

Ahiga appreciated that humility. He, too, lacked adequate words. "Lights" and "objects" were approximations, attempts to categorize something that exceeded categories. Were they physical? They'd seemed physical—he could see them, they moved through space, they responded to his presence. Were they spiritual? They'd felt spiritual—holy, purposeful, emanating that peace he associated with God's presence.

Maybe the question itself was wrong. Maybe physical and spiritual weren't as separate as modern thinking assumed. Maybe spiritual beings could manipulate physical reality, appear in forms that seemed technological but were simply their nature.

***

Over the following year or so, Ahiga integrated the experience into his faith without letting it dominate. He didn't become obsessed with UFOs or start a ministry based on his encounter. He simply allowed it to deepen his existing relationship with God, making him more attentive to guidance, more grateful for protection, more aware that reality contained dimensions he couldn't fully perceive.

He made one significant decision: he moved back to the reservation, took a job teaching at the tribal school, and reconnected with the land and community that had shaped him. The encounter hadn't dictated this choice—he'd been considering it before the lights appeared. But it had clarified his thinking, helped him see what mattered.

He led prayer walks occasionally, teaching others—

especially young Navajo Christians navigating the same cultural tensions he'd experienced—to be attentive to God's presence in creation. He never guaranteed anyone would see lights. Most didn't. But several reported experiences of guidance: sudden intuitions to change paths, unexplained feelings that led them away from danger, moments of profound peace in the wilderness when they'd felt lost or afraid.

Now, when students or church members ask Ahiga about angels, he tells them this: "Angels in the Bible appear as men, as fire, as light, as clouds, as stars. They take whatever form serves God's purpose. If you see something in the sky you can't explain, don't automatically assume it's hostile. Test it by the fruit: Does it lead toward God or away? Does it help or harm?"

"The lights led me away from death toward life. They appeared when I was seeking God in prayer. They vanished once their work was done. By those measures, I know whose servants they were—even if I can't explain how they moved or what they were made of."

He pauses, looking out his window toward the desert visible in the distance. "Our ancestors saw sacred things we modern people have explained away. Maybe some of those explanations are right. But maybe some are wrong. Maybe the desert still speaks to those who have ears to hear. Maybe the lights still guide those who need guidance."

"I don't claim to have all the answers. I just know that one night, when I needed help, heaven answered. And I'm alive today because I followed lights I couldn't explain toward safety I didn't know I needed."

The desert remains for Ahiga what it has always been: a place of prayer, testing, and encounter. He walks it regularly, sometimes alone, sometimes with students or family. He never seeks the lights—he learned that lesson. They appeared when needed, not when wanted. But he remains attentive, aware that thin places exist where heaven touches earth, and the desert is one of them.

The land speaks to those who listen. The lights guide those who follow. And the same God who led Israel with a pillar of fire still manifests His care in ways both ancient and immediate, both mysterious and unmistakably present.

REFLECTION

Ahiga Tsosie's encounter echoes one of Scripture's most sustained miraculous phenomena: the pillar of cloud and fire that guided Israel through the wilderness. This wasn't a one-time vision but a consistent presence, appearing night after night for forty years, leading thousands of people through hostile terrain (Exodus 13:21-22).

Think about what the text describes: an intelligent light that moved with purpose, stopped when the people needed to camp, resumed when it was time to travel, and provided both guidance and protection. It wasn't natural—clouds don't glow at night, fire doesn't form into columns that persist without fuel. It was supernatural, yes, but it was also... functional. Practical. Almost technological in its reliability.

Modern people read these accounts and immediately spiritualize them: "It represents God's presence," we say, as if the representation is all that matters. But the Israelites

Lights in the Sky

experienced something concrete enough to navigate by. They followed a real phenomenon, visible to everyone, predictable in its behavior yet clearly not natural.

What would such a phenomenon look like to modern eyes? A sustained aerial light, hovering over a specific location, moving with intelligent guidance, visible at night? It would look remarkably like what Ahiga described.

This doesn't mean every UFO is the pillar of fire reborn. But it does suggest we shouldn't be too quick to dismiss phenomena that share characteristics with biblical manifestations of divine presence.

The pillar served multiple purposes: it guided (showing direction), it protected (standing between Israel and Egypt's army in Exodus 14:19-20), and it manifested God's presence (making His nearness tangible). These same functions appear in Ahiga's account: the lights guided him away from danger, protected him from death, and created awareness of divine presence.

Scripture emphasizes that the pillar moved "at the Lord's command" (Numbers 9:18-23). When it moved, Israel moved. When it stopped, they camped. This created absolute dependence on divine guidance—they couldn't predict its movements, couldn't control when they traveled or rested. They had to watch, pay attention, and respond immediately.

Ahiga experienced something similar. The voice said "Walk" and his body responded before conscious thought could intervene. He followed without knowing the destination, trusting the lights' guidance even when it led him off trail into unfamiliar terrain. That kind of immediate obedience requires recognizing divine authority—something in Ahiga knew these lights could be trusted, even when rationality protested.

The canyon represents death averted. Without the lights, Ahiga would have walked over the edge. With them, he stopped three feet short. The margin was thin—a few more seconds of walking would have been fatal. But that's often how divine protection works in Scripture: not creating impossible distance between danger and deliverance, but providing exactly enough intervention at precisely the right moment.

Think of the Red Sea parting—not days before Israel arrived, but just in time (Exodus 14:21-22). Or the ravens feeding Elijah—not stockpiling food, but bringing it morning and evening as needed (1 Kings 17:4-6). Or Jesus feeding the five thousand—not preventing hunger, but satisfying it when it reached its peak (Matthew 14:15-21).

Divine intervention often operates on the edge, at the last moment, with just enough provision. This isn't divine negligence—it's intentional design. When help comes at the last possible moment, there's no mistaking it for coincidence or human effort. The timing itself testifies to intentionality.

Consider the star that guided the Magi (Matthew 2:9-10). Astronomer's have proposed various explanations—planetary conjunction, comet, supernova—but none adequately explain how a celestial object could "stop over the place where the child was." Whatever the Magi followed, it moved with intelligence similar to what Ahiga described: purposeful guidance toward a specific destination, stopping when the goal was reached.

Lights in the Sky

The early church father Origen suggested the star was an angel taking visible form to guide the Magi. That may be speculation, but it's biblically grounded speculation. Angels repeatedly appear as light (Luke 2:9), can move through space at will (Daniel 9:21), and serve as guides for God's people.

Elijah's transportation involved "chariots of fire and horses of fire" (2 Kings 2:11). These weren't metaphors—Elisha saw them clearly enough to cry out specific descriptions. Something visible, dramatic, involving fire and movement, carried Elijah away to heaven. Whether we call them angels or something else, they were real enough to be observed and described.

The Navajo context adds another layer. Ahiga's pastor's great grandfather saw similar lights during the Long Walk—one of the darkest chapters in Native American history. When the U.S. Army forced the Navajo from their homeland in 1864, thousands died during the 300-mile march to imprisonment. Those who survived did so through combination of endurance, mutual support, and—as some testimonies suggest—unexpected help.

That his great grandfather would pray "to Jesus and the Holy People both" reflects the synthesis many Native Christians developed: acknowledging Christ as Lord while recognizing that their ancestors had genuine encounters with divine realities, even if they named them differently.

Romans 1:20 states: "Since the creation of the world God's invisible qualities—his eternal power and divine nature—have been clearly seen, being understood from what has been made." This suggests God revealed Himself to all peoples in some measure, even before the Gospel reached them. The Navajo understanding of Holy People—spiritual beings connected to creation and the Creator—may have been their way of perceiving genuine angelic activity.

When Christianity arrived, some missionaries insisted all traditional beliefs were demonic. But more thoughtful missionaries recognized elements of truth in Native spirituality: belief in a Creator, awareness of spiritual beings, understanding that creation has sacred dimensions. These weren't contradictions of Christianity but preparation for it—God revealing Himself through creation and conscience before revealing Himself fully in Christ.

Ahiga navigates this tension thoughtfully. He doesn't equate Navajo tradition with biblical revelation, but neither does he dismiss it completely. He recognizes that the same God who sent angels to Israel could have sent them to his ancestors, and that cultural frameworks shape how people interpret and describe what they encounter.

This both/and approach reflects biblical wisdom. Paul in Athens acknowledged that the Greeks already worshiped God, however imperfectly, and then pointed them toward fuller truth in Christ (Acts 17:22-31). He didn't say "Everything you believed was demonic." He said "What you worship in ignorance, I declare to you."

Similarly, Ahiga can say: "My ancestors saw divine manifestations and called them Holy People. The Bible describes similar manifestations and calls them angels. Maybe they're the same thing, and God simply used different cultural languages to communicate the same reality."

This doesn't mean all spiritual experiences — even experienced by someone who is Navajo — are valid or all religions are equal. It means God can work within various cultural frameworks, revealing truth in ways people can receive it, while still calling all people ultimately to Christ as the full revelation of God (John 14:6).

The practical implications matter. If angels—or whatever divine agents God employs—still manifest in visible form, still guide people in danger, still respond to prayer, then we should:

1. Remain open to unusual experiences, testing them biblically rather than automatically dismissing them
2. Recognize that God's methods may not match our expectations or cultural assumptions
3. Hold mystery with respect, acknowledging that not everything can or should be fully explained
4. Stay grounded in Scripture as our authority while remaining open to how God might work outside our neat categories

Ahiga's story doesn't prove all UFO sightings are angels. It suggests that some encounters—especially those occurring during prayer, leading people toward safety and deeper faith—might be exactly what ancient people called angels: messengers of God, manifesting in forms that serve their purpose.

The desert still speaks. The lights still guide. The same God who led Israel with fire and cloud remains active, creative, and sovereign over all His creation—including the parts we don't yet understand.

TESTIMONY 4
THE FISHERMAN'S LIGHT

THE PACIFIC COAST of Washington is a study in contrasts—rocky beaches giving way to dense forest, waves crashing with relentless power, fog rolling in to blanket everything in pray silence. Jason Anderson had fished these waters for thirty-seven years, knew every inlet and current, every seasonal shift in the salmon runs.

He wasn't a particularly religious man. His wife attended church and prayed before meals; Jason gave thanks too, mostly out of habit, but didn't think much about God beyond that. The ocean was his cathedral—vast, powerful, indifferent. It demanded respect but offered no comfort, no promises beyond the cold equation of skill versus luck.

Jason had grown up on these waters. His father ran a charter fishing business out of Westport, and Jason spent his childhood learning the trade: how to read weather patterns, how to navigate by landmarks when fog obscured everything, how to find schools of fish by reading water temperature and bird activity. By fifteen, he could pilot the boat alone. By twenty, he'd bought his own vessel—a modest twenty-six-foot fishing boat he named *Sarah's Promise* after his grandmother.

The ocean taught hard lessons. Jason had seen boats go down in storms, watched friends lose fingers to winches, attended too many memorial services for fishermen who simply never came home. The sea gave and the sea took away, and you accepted both with the same stoic pragmatism. You did your job carefully, maintained your equipment, respected the weather, and hoped that would be enough.

Religion seemed irrelevant to that equation. Jason figured if God existed, He was busy with more important things than watching out for small-time fishermen. Prayer felt like superstition, something his wife did that made her feel better but didn't appear to actually change random outcomes. The ocean operated by its own laws—wind, current, temperature—and those laws didn't care whether you prayed or not.

His wife, coincidentally named Sarah like his boat, had never pushed him about faith. She attended the small Methodist church in town, sang in the choir, volunteered at community meals. Jason would show up for Christmas and Easter, sit in the back pew, and count the minutes until he could return to work. Sarah prayed for him—he knew that—but she didn't nag or lecture.

"The Lord will find you when He's ready," she'd say. "And you'll listen when you're ready."

It was September, late enough that tourist boats had thinned but early enough that weather remained mostly calm. Jason had taken his boat out alone—something Sarah hated but he'd done countless times. He planned to check his crab pots near the entrance to Grays Harbor, then head in before sunset. A routine day, or so he thought.

The morning went normally. Decent haul in the pots, good weather, the rhythmic work of pulling lines and checking traps. Jason worked methodically, his mind half on the task, half on the repairs he needed to make to the dock when he got home. Around 3 PM, he started the engine and pointed the bow toward harbor.

That's when the fog rolled in.

Pacific fog is different from other fog—thicker, wetter, faster-moving. It can blanket miles of ocean in minutes, turning a clear day into complete disorientation. Jason had navigated fog before, many times. He relied on GPS, radar, depth sounder, and thirty-seven years of experience reading water and wind.

But this fog was worse than usual. Visibility dropped to near zero within minutes—that thick, gray soup that erases the horizon, the shoreline, everything beyond twenty feet. Jason slowed to minimum speed and checked his electronics.

GPS screen: black. Radar: dead. Even the radio cut out mid-transmission.

Jason tried the standard troubleshooting: checked connections, flipped breakers, restarted systems. Nothing. Every electronic system had failed simultaneously—GPS, radar, radio, even his backup handheld GPS wouldn't power on, though the battery was fresh.

Now he was concerned. The harbor entrance was tricky even in good conditions—rocks on both sides, strong currents, shallow bars that shifted with every winter storm. In fog this thick, without electronics, attempting the entrance was dangerous. But staying outside in worsening conditions wasn't much better.

He killed the engine and drifted, listening. Experienced fishermen can sometimes navigate by sound—the pitch and rhythm of surf changes depending on proximity to shore, depth, and obstacles. But the fog dampened everything, made distance impossible to judge.

Jason tried to recall his exact position when the electronics died. He'd been roughly three miles northwest of the entrance, angling in. Current would push him south and east, but how fast? Wind was from the northwest, maybe eight knots, which would also push him east but more slowly than current. If he drifted for an hour, he might be past the entrance entirely, pushed toward the rocks south of the jetty.

Without instruments, he was navigating by dead reckoning—the old-fashioned method of estimating position based on speed, time, and direction. It worked when you had reference points or could see stars. In dense fog with no visibility, it was guesswork.

It was then he found himself praying, A three word prayer. "God help me." Followed by one word. "Jesus."

He'd been drifting perhaps twenty minutes when he saw the light.

It appeared off his port bow, hovering about fifteen feet above the water. At first he thought it was another boat's spotlight, but the position was wrong—no mast, no hull visible below the light. And the glow itself was strange: golden-white, soft-edged, not the harsh beam of a searchlight.

The light pulsed once—bright enough to illuminate the fog around it—then moved forward slowly, paralleling his boat about thirty yards out.

Jason stared, trying to make sense of it. Another vessel? But no navigation lights, no engine sound, no wake or disturbance in the water. Helicopter? No rotor wash, no sound. A buoy? Buoys don't hover above the water, don't move.

The light pulsed again, brighter this time. And Jason had the strangest impression—not words, not audible, but a clear sense of invitation. Almost hearing *Follow me* though no voice spoke.

He hesitated. Every rational instinct screamed this was wrong. You don't follow random lights in fog. You don't make navigation decisions based on unexplained phenomena. But something deeper—call it intuition, call it desperation, call it something else entirely—made him restart his engine.

He pointed the bow toward the light and advanced slowly, throttle barely engaged, keeping the mysterious glow just in sight through the fog.

The light led him forward, maintaining consistent distance. When Jason adjusted speed, the light adjusted too, always staying visible but never close enough to touch or identify. It moved with obvious intelligence, occasionally shifting position to keep him on what felt like a specific course.

Once, the light stopped abruptly. Jason cut his engine immediately, and in the sudden silence he heard it: waves breaking over rocks, close—too close. Maybe twenty feet off his starboard side. Without the light's warning, he'd have drifted directly into them. The light pulsed twice, as if saying *yes, you hear it*, then moved right, leading him around the hazard he couldn't see but could now hear clearly.

Time became strange. Jason felt like he'd been following the light for hours, but checking his watch (one of the few instruments still working) showed only fifteen minutes had passed. The fog remained thick as cotton, visibility near zero, yet he felt no panic. Just strange calm, trust in the light ahead, certainty that he was being guided by something that knew these waters better than he did.

Then, gradually, the fog began to thin. Tendrils of it lifted, revealing glimpses of darker water, then suddenly breaking entirely. Jason found himself perhaps fifty yards from the harbor entrance, lined up perfectly with the channel between the jetties. The familiar markers emerged from the mist—the south jetty's warning beacon, the red channel marker, the entrance lights.

The mysterious light hovered one final time, pulsed so bright Jason had to shield his eyes, then shot straight up and vanished into the remaining fog overhead. One moment it was there, solid and real; the next, gone completely.

His electronics blinked back to life. GPS screen glowed, showing his exact position. Radar swept its circular pattern, painting the jetties and shoreline. Radio crackled with Coast Guard traffic. Every system suddenly functional, as if they'd never failed.

Jason sat motionless for perhaps thirty seconds, hands gripping the wheel, heart pounding. Then he engaged the engine and piloted slowly through the entrance, between the familiar jetties, into the protected harbor. His hands shook on the wheel. His breath came in short gasps. But he was home, safe, alive.

He tied up at his usual slip, checked his equipment thoroughly. Nothing was wrong. No blown fuses, no loose connections, no water damage to electronics. The systems worked perfectly, as if they'd never stopped.

***

Jason started attending church with Sarah—first reluctantly, then with genuine interest. The hymns and prayers that had once seemed empty now resonated differently. When the congregation sang "Amazing Grace"—*I once was lost but now am found, was blind but now I see*—Jason felt the words in his chest. He'd been lost in fog. Something had found him.

The pastor, hearing his story during a private counseling session, pulled out a Bible and turned to Exodus 13:21: "By day the Lord went ahead of them in a pillar of cloud to guide them on their way and by night in a pillar of fire to give them light, so that they could travel by day or night."

"You were lost in fog," the pastor said. "God sent a light to guide you home. Why does that seem more impossible than what He did for Israel?"

Jason had no answer to that. He'd spent thirty-seven years on the ocean, trusting in skill and equipment. But when everything failed, when he faced disaster alone in the fog, something else had intervened. Something that cared whether he lived or died. Something with the power to guide him through impossible circumstances.

He began reading Scripture seriously for the first time since childhood. The stories of divine guidance—the pillar of fire, the star leading the Magi, angels appearing with specific instructions—took on new weight. These weren't fairy tales or metaphors. They were accounts of God breaking into ordinary situations with practical help.

Lights in the Sky

The pillar of fire particularly resonated. It appeared to people who were lost, provided guidance they couldn't manage themselves, led them safely through dangerous territory. That was exactly what Jason had experienced: a light in darkness, guidance through danger, safe passage to harbor.

Jason told his story to other fishermen, carefully. Most nodded politely but clearly thought he'd panicked in the fog, followed the wrong light, gotten lucky. A few, usually older men, shared their own experiences: lights seen during storms, voices heard warning them away from danger, moments when disaster loomed and something inexplicable intervened.

One Japanese-American fisherman, a man in his seventies who rarely spoke about his past, told Jason about his grandfather during World War II. "He was in the internment camp, tried to escape, got lost in the desert. He said lights appeared in the sky and led him to a road where someone picked him up. He survived because he followed them. Always believed they were angels. Family thought he'd had heatstroke, but he never changed his story."

The pattern was consistent across stories: people in crisis, lights appearing, guidance provided, lives saved. And almost everyone kept quiet about it, fearing ridicule or disbelief.

Jason became more open about his faith and his experience. He spoke at his church, then at other churches along the coast. Not preaching—just telling his story: "I was lost. A light guided me home. Maybe it was an angel. Maybe it was something else. But I know this: I should be dead, and I'm not. Something out there cared enough to save me."

His boat now carries a small plaque near the wheel: "Psalm 107:29-30 - He stilled the storm to a whisper; the waves of the sea were hushed. They were glad when it grew calm, and he guided them to their desired haven."

Sometimes, heading out in early morning or returning at dusk, Jason sees lights moving over the water—distant, quick, gone before he can focus on them. He doesn't chase them or try to photograph them. He just whispers "Thank you" and continues his work.

Because whether they're angels or something else entirely, he knows they serve the same God who calmed storms for the disciples, who guides the lost, who cares about ordinary fishermen getting home safely to their families.

The ocean remains vast and powerful and sometimes deadly. But Jason no longer sees it as indifferent. He sees it as God's creation, inhabited by God's servants, watched over by the One who "set the boundaries of the sea" (Jeremiah 5:22) and still guides those who call out to Him in their distress.

Several years after his encounter, Jason encountered a marine biologist at the harbor who was studying unusual bioluminescence patterns. Jason mentioned his experience cautiously, wondering if he'd seen some natural phenomenon - understanding that even if that was what it was, it was still a miracle, appearing in answer to prayer guiding him specifically home.

. The scientist listened, then shook her head.

"Bioluminescence doesn't behave like that," she said. "It doesn't hover above water, doesn't move in coordinated patterns, doesn't respond to human presence. What you're describing... I don't have an explanation for that."

She paused, then added quietly: "But I've heard similar stories. Not often, but regularly enough. Fishermen see things. Most don't report it because we scientists would just dismiss them. But off the record? There's something out there. Call it what you want."

Jason appreciated her honesty. He wasn't looking for scientific validation—he knew what he'd experienced. But hearing a scientist acknowledge that some phenomena exceed current explanations helped him feel less isolated.

He learned that other fishing communities reported similar experiences. Japanese fishermen spoke of *hitodama* (soul-lights) that sometimes guided boats to safety. Irish fishermen told stories of mysterious lights off the coast, traditionally attributed to spirits but often benevolent. Even ancient maritime cultures—Greek, Phoenician, Polynesian—recorded accounts of guiding lights appearing during storms.

Were all these stories about the same phenomenon? Jason couldn't say. But the pattern was global and historical: mariners in distress, mysterious lights, guidance to safety. Different cultures interpreted them through different frameworks—spirits, gods, ancestors, saints. But perhaps they were all describing the same reality: divine messengers manifesting to help those who work dangerous waters.

Jason's own faith deepened steadily. He joined a men's prayer group at church, led Bible studies for other fishermen, and became known in the community as someone willing to talk openly about spiritual matters.

His testimony always included the caveat: "I can't prove what I saw was an angel. I just know I was guided by something beyond human technology, something that cared whether I lived or died. And that showed up after I called on the name of Jesus."

The practical impact showed in his approach to fishing. He still prepared carefully, maintained equipment rigorously, and respected weather patterns. But he also prayed before every trip—not vague prayers, but specific requests for safety, guidance, and protection. And he found himself more attentive to intuition, to subtle promptings that suggested changing course or checking equipment.

Twice in the years following his encounter, Jason felt sudden urges to alter his route. Both times, he later learned he'd avoided hazards: once a semi-submerged log that would have damaged his propeller, once a sudden squall that hit the area he'd been heading toward. Were these divine warnings or good instincts? He couldn't prove either way, but he'd learned to listen.

Sarah watched her husband's transformation with quiet joy. The man who'd sat impatiently through Christmas services now led prayer meetings. The skeptic who'd dismissed her faith now shared testimony openly. It was beyond all the women in her prayer group had hoped for when they'd pleaded to God for his salvation.

"God's been pursuing you for thirty-seven years," she told him. "He just needed the right moment to get your attention."

"Took a crisis," Jason admitted. "And a mysterious light. And electronic failure. But He got me."

Now in his sixties, Jason still fishes regularly, though his son has taken over most of the charter business. He remains a familiar presence at the harbour—weathered, practical, not given to mysticism or exaggeration. Which is exactly why his story carries weight. When Jason Anderson says he was guided by a mysterious light, other fishermen listen. Because if it happened to someone that solid, that experienced, that skeptical... maybe it could happen to anyone.

The harbor community has quietly acknowledged that strange things happen on the water. Not supernatural in the sensational sense, but unexplained. Fishermen go missing and are found alive days later with stories of guidance they can't explain. Boats avoid collisions in ways the survivors attribute to "instinct" but can't fully account for. Equipment fails and restarts at crucial moments.

Jason doesn't claim all these incidents are angelic. But he's stopped dismissing them automatically. "The ocean's bigger than we know," he tells younger fishermen. "And God's bigger than the ocean. If He wants to send help, He'll send it in whatever form works. Our job is to pay attention and be grateful."

REFLECTION

Jason Anderson's encounter raises the question many Christians avoid: Does God still intervene directly in physical circumstances? Not through human agency or natural processes, but through supernatural manifestation—lights, voices, beings that appear precisely when needed then vanish once their work is done?

Theologically, most Christians would say "Of course God can intervene." But practically, we've created categories that make modern miracles suspect while ancient miracles remain comfortably distant. We believe God parted the Red Sea but struggle to believe He might guide a fisherman through fog with a light that defies natural explanation.

Yet Scripture's accounts of divine guidance are startlingly physical and practical. The pillar of fire and cloud didn't just symbolize God's presence—it provided actual navigation for millions of people crossing hostile terrain (Exodus 13:21-22). The guidance wasn't metaphorical. It was concrete: follow this light at night, this cloud by day, and you'll survive the wilderness.

The star that led the Magi wasn't allegorical—it moved, stopped, and indicated a specific location (Matthew 2:9-10). Whatever they followed, it behaved with obvious intelligence, guiding them across hundreds of miles to a precise destination.

When Peter needed rescuing from prison, an angel produced actual light that woke him, struck physical chains that fell off, and opened real doors (Acts 12:6-10). This wasn't spiritual experience happening in Peter's heart—it was tangible intervention that solved a practical problem.

These accounts share characteristics:
- Crisis situations where human ability proved insufficient
- Divine intervention manifesting in physical, observable ways
- Practical guidance or help rather than merely symbolic presence
- Witnesses left with both gratitude and awe
- Outcomes that preserved life or furthered God's purposes

Jason's experience fits this pattern. He faced genuine danger—lost in fog, electronics failed, unable to navigate safely. Divine help came in observable form—a light that moved with obvious intelligence. The guidance was practical—leading him around hazards, through safe channels, to harbor. The outcome preserved life and transformed faith.

The key difference between Jason's experience and some other UFO encounters lies in the fruit. Many abduction accounts describe trauma, violation, terror, and lasting psychological damage. These bear none of the hallmarks of biblical angelic encounters, which typically begin with "Do not be afraid" (said more than 80 times in Scripture) and leave people blessed rather than broken.

Biblical angels do startle and overwhelm—their appearances often terrify initially. But the terror comes from encountering holy power, not from malevolent intent. Once angels identify themselves and state their purpose, fear gives way to worship (of God, never of them) or obedience. The encounter leaves witnesses changed but not damaged, awed but not traumatized.

Jason's experience followed this pattern: initial confusion, then profound peace, then guidance that saved his life, then lasting transformation toward God. No trauma. No obsession with the phenomenon. No repeated seeking of similar experiences. Just gratitude, deepened faith, and commitment to share what happened without becoming defined by it.

Some will argue that what Jason saw must have been a human source—Coast Guard boat, lighthouse beam refracted through fog, some explainable phenomenon. But

Jason is an experienced sailor who knows what Coast Guard boats sound like, how lighthouse beams behave, how fog affects light. The light he followed moved silently, hovered impossibly, responded to his position, and vanished instantaneously when its purpose was accomplished.

Could God have used a natural means? Certainly. God often works through ordinary circumstances (and it can still be a 'miracle' when in answer to prayer. But sometimes—as Scripture demonstrates repeatedly—He works through means that transcend natural explanation. And when those means appear, we shouldn't feel compelled to rationalize them away just because they make us uncomfortable.

The pillar of fire guiding Israel would look remarkably like a UFO to modern eyes: an intelligently controlled light source, hovering, moving with purpose, visible to thousands of witnesses. If it appeared today, our first instinct wouldn't be "That's God guiding His people." We'd immediately reach for technological explanations, dismiss religious interpretations as primitive thinking.

Perhaps that's our loss. Perhaps we've become so naturalistic that we've lost the ancient awareness that spiritual beings actively operate in physical space. Angels in Scripture don't just whisper inspiration—they roll away stones (Matthew 28:2), strike enemies dead (2 Kings 19:35), shut lions' mouths (Daniel 6:22), and yes, guide people with light (Acts 12:7).

Why wouldn't they still do such things? Hebrews 1:14 describes angels as "ministering spirits sent to serve those who will inherit salvation"—present tense, ongoing role, not past accomplishment. If they're still sent to serve, and if serving sometimes requires physical intervention, why wouldn't we expect such interventions to continue?

The maritime context is significant. Throughout history, seafarers have reported unusual guidance during crises. This isn't just Christian testimony—it's cross-cultural and historical. Something about working dangerous waters seems to make people more attentive to help from unexpected sources.

Perhaps the vulnerability of being on the ocean—far from land, subject to forces beyond control, aware of human limitation—creates receptivity to divine assistance. Or perhaps God particularly watches over those who work environments where death lurks constantly, where human skill can only go so far, where humility comes naturally.

Psalm 107:23-30 specifically addresses sailors: "Some went out on the sea in ships... They saw the works of the Lord, his wonderful deeds in the deep... He stilled the storm to a whisper; the waves of the sea were hushed. They were glad when it grew calm, and he guided them to their desired haven."

This psalm was written thousands of years ago, yet it describes exactly what Jason experienced: going out on the sea, encountering danger, being guided to safe haven. The pattern is ancient, biblical, and apparently ongoing.

Jason returned to that psalm repeatedly after his encounter. He'd read it before without thinking much about it—just poetic language about God's power. Now he understood it as testimony, as someone recording actual experience of divine guidance at sea.

"He guided them to their desired haven"—that's not

metaphor. That's navigation. That's a light in the fog showing the way home.

Perhaps the real miracle isn't that such things happen, but that we've convinced ourselves they shouldn't. Perhaps God's creativity in helping His children exceeds our categories. Perhaps the lights still guide, the angels still minister, and heaven still intervenes—if we have eyes to see and humility to accept help in whatever form it comes.

Jason Anderson will tell you he doesn't understand everything about what happened that day. He can't explain the technology (if it was technology) or the mechanism (if there was one). He also can't explain why not every lost fisherman is rescued. He simply testifies: "I was lost in fog. I prayed. Called on Jesus. A light guided me home. I'm alive because I followed it. And I'll spend the rest of my life grateful to the One who sent that light, whatever it was."

That gratitude transformed him. Not into a mystic or UFO enthusiast, but into a man more aware of God's presence, more attentive to guidance, more certain that we're never truly alone on dangerous waters.

The ocean remains vast. But it's God's ocean. And His messengers still watch over those who work it, appearing when needed in whatever form serves their purpose—even if that form looks to modern eyes more like advanced technology than traditional angels.

TESTIMONY 5
THE MOUNTAIN WATCHERS

CHARLES AND PATRICIA HOFFMAN had been married for thirty-two years. They'd raised three children, survived financial struggles, weathered the normal storms of long marriage. Camping in the Cascade Mountains had been their escape for decades—a chance to reconnect away from phones, schedules, and the noise of suburban life.

The Hoffmans weren't adventurers by temperament. Charles worked as an insurance adjuster, Patricia as an elementary school teacher. Their camping trips were carefully planned affairs: well-maintained equipment, detailed itineraries shared with their adult children. They weren't seekers of thrills or mystical experiences. They simply enjoyed the peace of the mountains, the smell of pine, the sound of creeks tumbling over rocks.

That June found them at their favorite camping spot near Mount Rainier, accessible only by a rough forest service road that deterred most casual campers. They'd been coming to this spot for fifteen years, knew every trail, every viewpoint, every quirk of the terrain. The familiarity was part of the appeal—a place so known it required no mental effort, just presence and rest.

They arrived Friday evening, set up their tent with practiced efficiency, enjoyed a simple dinner over the campfire. The only ones there. The forest was quiet, peaceful, broken only by occasional owl calls and the distant sound of a creek they'd swim in tomorrow. Patricia read while Charles organized their gear for the next day's hike. Around ten PM, they retired to the tent, exhausted from the week and the drive.

Around midnight, Patricia woke suddenly. Not from a dream or sound, but from an overwhelming sense of being watched. She lay still, listening. Charles snored softly beside her. The forest outside was silent—too silent, she realized. No insects. No wind. Not even the creek she'd heard earlier.

The silence pressed against the tent fabric like a physical presence, dense and expectant. Patricia's heart began to pound, primal awareness flooding her nervous system with adrenaline. Something was out there. She didn't know how she knew, but she knew with absolute certainty.

Then she saw the lights through the tent fabric.

Not flashlights—the glow was wrong, too diffuse, too golden. And they were moving in patterns overhead, visible through the thin nylon. Patricia unzipped the tent flap carefully, not wanting to wake Charles but unable to stay inside, drawn by curiosity stronger than caution.

Three lights hovered above the clearing where they'd pitched their tent. Large—each maybe six feet across—geometric in shape but somehow organic in movement. Not perfect circles but shifting forms that her eyes couldn't quite hold, shapes that seemed to rotate through dimensions she couldn't perceive. They pulsed gently, creating patterns that Patricia's mind struggled to follow. Not random. Intentional. Almost... communicative, like watching someone sign in a language you don't speak but recognize as language.

She should have been terrified. Later, she'd wonder at her

own calmness. But in the moment, she felt profound peace, the same sensation she'd experienced during pivotal moments of prayer—her wedding day, the births of her children, the night her mother died when Patricia had knelt beside the hospital bed and felt surrounded by love despite grief.

"Chuck!" she whispered, reaching back into the tent to shake him. "Chuck, wake up."

He stirred, grumbling, then sat up abruptly when he saw her silhouetted against the strange light. "What the—"

They sat at the tent opening for perhaps twenty minutes, watching the lights perform their geometric dance. Neither spoke. Words felt inadequate, almost sacrilegious. The lights moved in coordinated patterns: forming triangles, dissolving into lines, creating interlocking circles, then shifting to configurations Patricia couldn't name because geometry didn't have terms for them. Three-dimensional patterns rotating through space, or perhaps four-dimensional patterns rotating through time, glimpses of structure too complex for human perception to fully grasp.

The forest remained absolutely silent. Not even their own breathing seemed to make sound, as if they'd been enclosed in a bubble where normal acoustic laws didn't apply. The air felt different—charged, expectant, almost solid.

Then the lights began ascending, slowly at first, maintaining their formation. They rose straight up through the canopy—Patricia distinctly saw branches sway as something passed through them, though the lights seemed to move through matter as easily as through air. They ascended perhaps two hundred feet, paused, pulsed brilliantly in unison, and shot straight up with acceleration that defied physics. One moment they were there, clear and visible; the next, gone, vanished into the night sky as if they'd never existed.

The forest sounds returned immediately: insects resuming mid-chirp, wind rustling through pine needles, the distant creek gurgling over rocks. As if someone had unmuted the world.

Charles and Patricia looked at each other in the sudden darkness, eyes adjusting, neither quite believing what they'd witnessed.

"Did we just—" Charles started.

"Yes," Patricia said.

They didn't sleep the rest of the night. They rebuilt the fire they'd let die earlier, sat wrapped in blankets, watching the sky, occasionally glancing at each other with expressions that mixed awe, confusion, and something like joy. Not the giddy happiness of winning the lottery, but the deep joy of glimpsing something that confirmed the world was larger than they'd imagined.

When dawn came, they walked the clearing carefully. No burn marks, no physical evidence, no flattened vegetation. But Patricia noticed something: the wild strawberries around the campsite—which had been small and green yesterday when she'd checked them, planning to pick some in a few days when they ripened—were suddenly ripe. Impossibly ripe, as if they'd matured overnight instead of over the week such ripening normally required.

"Plants don't do that," Charles said. He'd taught high school biology for thirty years before retiring. "That's not possible. Ripening requires days of chemical processes, sugar accumulation, cell wall breakdown. You can't accelerate it overnight."

Patricia picked one, tasted it. Sweet, perfect, fully ripe. She looked up at where the lights had hovered. "None of this is possible."

* * *

They didn't report their experience to authorities. Who would they tell? They figured park rangers would file it under "strange camper stories" and forget it. UFO researchers would descend with questionnaires and equipment, turning their private encounter into public spectacle. The Hoffmans had no desire for attention or investigation. Patricia also admitted she was afraid of a potential visitor from the Men in Black of UFO lore.

But they couldn't shake what they'd witnessed. The peace they'd felt was too real, too tangible. It had been like standing in a cathedral during the most sacred moment of worship—that sense of transcendence that makes you feel small yet somehow precious, that awareness of participating in something vast and beautiful.

Patricia, who'd grown up Catholic, found herself returning to Scripture with new eyes. She read about the transfiguration, where Jesus appeared in brilliant light before His disciples (Matthew 17:1-8). Peter, Charles, and John witnessed something so overwhelming they wanted to build shelters and stay there. They saw light that exceeded normal brightness, experienced presence that transcended ordinary reality. When it ended, they were changed—not traumatized, but transformed by having glimpsed divine glory.

She read about angels appearing to shepherds in fields, causing fear that required reassurance: "Do not be afraid" (Luke 2:8-10). The pattern was consistent: ordinary people encountering extraordinary manifestations, feeling both awe and peace, receiving messages or experiencing presence without always understanding what they'd witnessed.

Charles, more skeptical by nature and training, struggled with the experience. As a science teacher, he'd built his worldview on observable, testable phenomena. But he'd observed something he couldn't test or explain. The lights had been real—Patricia had seen them too, so it wasn't individual hallucination. They'd behaved with obvious intelligence, moved in ways that violated known physics. And those strawberries... he'd gone back the next morning to photograph them, still unable to believe plants had ripened overnight but knowing also even while doing so that he could not provide a photo from the day before to anyone else to show the transformation. Any skeptic would rightly say they could be early ripening. Or the fruit in the same area was at various different stages of growth. He realized it was only evidenced to himself and his wife. *They* knew how they had been.

He started researching historical accounts, not conspiracy websites but scholarly documentation. What he found surprised him: credible reports spanning centuries and cultures of lights behaving similarly. Native American accounts of "star people." Medieval chronicles describing "wheels of fire" in the sky. Japanese records of "flying boats"

Lights in the Sky

(*Utsuro-bune*). Australian Aboriginal stories of *min min* lights that appeared during ceremonies.

Across cultures, these lights were almost never described as hostile. They were watchers, guardians, sometimes teachers. They appeared to people during sacred activities—prayer, ceremony, times of need. The descriptions varied by cultural framework, but the core experience remained consistent: intelligent lights, peaceful presence, encounters that left witnesses awed rather than traumatized.

"What if," Charles asked Patricia one evening as they processed the experience, "what if UFO is just our modern word for what the ancients called angels? What if we've been seeing the same thing all along, but we interpret it through our cultural lens?"

The question opened new avenues of thought. Patricia began researching angelology—the theological study of angels. She discovered that Christian tradition had always understood angels as taking multiple forms: appearing as humans (Genesis 18-19), as frightening beings (Daniel 10:5-9), as lights (Luke 2:9), even as natural phenomena like wind or fire when serving God's purposes.

Thomas Aquinas wrote extensively about angelic abilities: they can move instantaneously, manipulate matter, appear in bodies temporarily assumed for specific purposes. They're not bound by human physics but can work within it when necessary. They exist primarily in the spiritual realm but can manifest physically.

If angels possess such abilities—and Scripture consistently portrays them as powerful, capable of dramatic physical interventions—why wouldn't their manifestations sometimes look technological?

The Hoffmans began attending church more regularly—a small congregation that had room for mystery in its theology, that didn't dismiss spiritual experiences as either delusion or demons. When the pastor asked if anyone had testimonies to share, Patricia cautiously stood and told their story. Not claiming to know what the lights were, just sharing what they'd experienced and saying she felt they were of God.

She expected skepticism or even hostility—some churches treated any unusual experience as demonic. Instead, an elderly woman approached her and Charles after service. "My husband saw them too," she said quietly. "Nineteen fifty-two, before we were married. He was camping alone in the Cascades. Lights appeared, moved above him for what seemed like hours. He said he felt God's presence stronger than he ever had in church... he swore they were angels."

Charles remained more cautious. "I can't prove they're angels," he said. "I can only testify to what we saw: intelligent lights, peaceful presence, and strawberries that shouldn't exist."

They returned to the same campsite the following summer, half hoping the lights would appear again, half dreading it. They didn't. The area looked ordinary, felt ordinary—no lingering sense of presence, no unusual phenomena. But the strawberry patch remained unusually abundant, producing fruit earlier and sweeter than any other wild strawberries in the area.

"Maybe that's the point," Patricia said, examining a handful of berries. "Not to give us spectacle every time we come back, but to leave us with evidence that something extraordinary happened. A reminder that the world is larger than we know."

Charles couldn't argue with that logic. The strawberries were real, tangible, testable—unlike the lights, which existed now only in memory and testimony. But those berries shouldn't be as lush as they were, shouldn't produce as early or as sweet. He'd tested the soil, checked the microclimate, compared them to similar patches nearby. No natural explanation accounted for their extraordinary productivity.

"God likes to leave calling cards," Patricia continued, picking another berry. "Evidence for those with eyes to see, mystery for those who aren't ready."

The Hoffmans now lead a small group for people who've had unusual spiritual experiences—encounters that don't fit neatly into categories, knowing they were lucky to find a church that didn't ridicule or ostracise them. They don't claim to explain everything. They simply provide safe space for "UFO witnesses" to share without judgment, to explore what their experiences might mean.

The group meets monthly, usually eight to twelve people. They open with prayer, then someone shares. Stories vary wildly. Each brings their story, their questions, their attempts to integrate extraordinary experience with ordinary faith.

"We saw lights we can't explain," Patricia tells newcomers. "We felt peace we'll never forget. We found strawberries that shouldn't exist. Those are the facts. What they mean... that's between each person and God. But we know this: we're not alone in experiencing the extraordinary. And we shouldn't let fear of seeming foolish keep us from acknowledging what we've witnessed either."

Charles adds, "Science teaches us to observe carefully and report honestly. Faith teaches us humility before mystery. Both are valuable. Both are necessary. And sometimes, they both point toward the same conclusion: something beyond our current understanding is at work in the world."

The group don't call themselves UFO believers or angel enthusiasts. They call themselves "witnesses"—people who saw something they can't fully explain but know was real, who choose to testify rather than hide, who trust that God is bigger than their categories and more creative than their theology allows.

Patricia ends with this thought: "We are all experiencers," she says mentioning the term used for those who have witnessed UFO activity. She pauses then adds: "… Experiencers of God's goodness." Pointing to the One behind the phenomenons more than the phenomenons itself.

Every June, the Hoffmans return to that campsite. They camp, pray, watch the stars, and remember the night the lights came. Whether angels or something else, those lights changed them—made them more open, more humble, more aware that creation is wild and wonderful and full of holy mysteries.

The strawberries still grow unusually sweet in that clearing. A small sign, but persistent. A reminder that when heaven touches earth, it leaves traces for those with eyes to see. Not proof that demands belief, but evidence that invites wonder—exactly the kind of sign God seems to prefer, leaving room for faith while providing enough substance that faith isn't blind.

Lights in the Sky

REFLECTION

The Hoffmans' experience illustrates a crucial principle often missed in discussions of unexplained phenomena: not everything needs immediate explanation. Sometimes mystery itself is the message, the invitation to humility and wonder that modern certainty has trained out of us.

Western Christianity has become uncomfortable with mystery. We want answers, categories, clear doctrinal positions on everything. We've created systematic theologies that attempt to explain God completely, leaving no room for "I don't know" or "This exceeds my understanding." Mystery feels like failure—intellectual laziness or spiritual immaturity.

But Scripture is full of unexplained mysteries. How did Jesus walk on water? (Matthew 14:25). How did He feed thousands with a few loaves? (Mark 6:41-44). How did He appear in a locked room after resurrection? (John 20:19). The Bible describes these events but doesn't explain the mechanism. It invites wonder rather than demanding understanding.

The Hoffmans didn't rush to label what they'd seen. They observed, they remembered, they tested it against Scripture and their own spiritual discernment. By the fruit—increased faith, deeper peace, sustained awe—they recognized it as something that drew them toward God rather than away from Him.

The overnight ripening of strawberries is fascinating precisely because it's both small and impossible. Not parting seas or raising the dead—miracles so dramatic they demand explanation. But acceleration of natural processes in ways that violate biology while leaving the fruit perfectly normal. Small enough to miss, impossible enough to remember.

This echoes biblical patterns of God leaving physical evidence. The budding of Aaron's staff (Numbers 17:8) proved his authority through impossible plant growth. Gideon's fleece, dry when the ground was wet (Judges 6:37-40), provided physical confirmation of spiritual encounter. These weren't dramatic enough to force belief, but substantial enough to sustain faith.

The strawberries serve the same function: ongoing evidence that something happened, subtle enough to be dismissed by skeptics, tangible enough to remind the Hoffmans their experience was real. Every June when they return and find that patch producing earlier and sweeter than it should, they're reminded: the lights were real, the encounter happened, the world contains more than they'd imagined.

The Hoffmans' approach to sharing their experience shows wisdom often lacking in these discussions. They didn't become evangelists for a UFO-angel theory. They didn't start a ministry claiming special revelation. They simply created space for others who'd experienced similar things— people who needed permission to acknowledge the extraordinary without being labeled crazy or heretical or having to of down New Age pathways to find understanding.

This addresses a real problem in many churches. Christians have encountered things they can't explain: answers to prayer that defy probability, healings without medical explanation, moments of guidance or protection

Lights in the Sky

that seem to involve unseen help, experiences during worship that felt like touching something beyond the material world. But they stay silent because speaking invites judgment, skepticism, or accusations of being deceived by demons.

Some will argue we shouldn't confuse UFO phenomena with angels, that the two are separate categories demanding separate explanations. But perhaps that distinction is more modern than biblical. Ancient people didn't have the category "extraterrestrial technology." When they saw lights in the sky moving with intelligence, they called them angels, messengers, chariots of fire, wheels within wheels.

Were they wrong? Or were they simply using the language they had to describe what they observed?

Consider: if angels exist (which orthodox Christianity affirms), if they're sent to minister to believers (Hebrews 1:14), if they can appear in forms ranging from human to overwhelming glory (Genesis 18-19; Daniel 10:5-9)—why wouldn't they sometimes appear as lights? Why wouldn't their movement seem technological to our eyes?

The Bible never limits angels to Renaissance painting aesthetics. It describes them as having power over nature (Revelation 7:1), moving with speed beyond human comprehension (Daniel 9:21), appearing in forms that terrify until they announce "Do not be afraid" (Luke 1:13, 2:10, Matthew 28:5).

If such beings appeared today, they'd likely be labeled UFOs before being recognized as angels. Our categories have changed, but perhaps the reality hasn't.

The crucial question remains: What is the fruit? Does an

encounter lead toward God or away from Him? Toward humility or pride? Toward worship or obsession? Toward integration with faith or replacement of it?

The Hoffmans' group provides a model for navigating this. They gather to share experiences, test them against Scripture, pray for discernment, and support each other in integration. They don't claim certainty about what they've seen, but they refuse to deny or diminish it. They hold mystery with both hands: respecting it enough not to force premature explanations, grounding themselves enough not to drift into speculation disconnected from biblical truth.

This approach—honoring mystery while maintaining discernment—reflects biblical wisdom better than either pure skepticism or uncritical acceptance. Paul writes about being "caught up to the third heaven" and hearing "inexpressible things, things that no one is permitted to tell" (2 Corinthians 12:2-4). He experienced something beyond his ability to fully describe or explain. Yet he testified to it, acknowledging both the reality and the mystery.

Perhaps that's where we need to land with phenomena like the Hoffmans witnessed: testifying honestly while remaining humble about our interpretations. Acknowledging that something happened while admitting we don't have complete understanding. Trusting that God is bigger than our categories and that His ways of manifesting to His children might exceed our theological boxes.

The strawberries still grow sweet in that clearing. A small miracle, but persistent. Not spectacular enough to force belief, substantial enough to sustain it. A reminder that when heaven touches earth—in whatever form, through whatever means—creation itself responds. The physical world bears the fingerprints of the spiritual, subtle signs for those with eyes to see and hearts open to wonder.

And those with such eyes and hearts can taste the evidence long after the lights have gone, recognizing that the world is larger, stranger, and more beautiful than our categories allow—exactly as God intended.

CONCLUSION
LIVING IN WONDER

These five accounts share threads difficult to dismiss: credible witnesses, physical effects, transformations that lead toward rather than away from God. None of the people in these stories sought publicity or profit. Most stayed silent for years, sharing only when they felt safe, when they found communities that could hold mystery without forcing premature explanations.

I began this book acknowledging it raises more questions than answers. That remains true. I don't know with certainty whether every phenomenon described here was angelic. I can't prove lights in the sky are always (or ever) divine messengers. I acknowledge some UFO encounters bear no resemblance to biblical angelophanies and likely have entirely different explanations.

But I've witnessed something consistent across these testimonies: fruit that passes biblical tests. Carl Peterson emerged more faithful, not less. Henry Caldwell's family farm prospered under apparent blessing. Ahiga Tsosie integrated his encounter into existing faith rather than being led astray. Jason Anderson moved from skepticism to worship. The Hoffmans created community for others wrestling with mystery.

These aren't marks of deception or delusion. They're marks of genuine encounter with the holy.

I'm not asking readers to accept my assessment

uncritically. I'm asking you to read carefully, think critically, peay for wisdom, and apply biblical discernment yourself.

I'm also asking you to remain open to possibility that angels—if they exist and remain active (which Scripture affirms in Hebrews 1:14, present tense)—might not always appear in forms we expect.

The real issue isn't whether UFOs are angels. It's whether we've become so naturalistic that we've lost ability to recognize supernatural activity when it occurs. We've explained away so much that we risk explaining away everything, leaving ourselves with faith that's theoretically orthodox but experientially empty.

Many believers struggle with this topic because it sits at uncomfortable intersections: faith and mystery, certainty and humility, caution and openness. We want clear answers. We want to know definitively whether phenomena are angelic, natural, or deceptive. But perhaps God allows some mystery to remain precisely because it requires us to exercise both faith and discernment, to hold tension without collapsing it into easy answers.

C.S. Lewis wrote in *Miracles*: "There is no reason to suppose that the frontiers between [the natural and supernatural] are stiff and fast, or that we know exactly where they run."

If spiritual beings can interact with physical reality, if angels can manipulate matter and energy, then boundaries between "spiritual" and "technological" become fuzzy.

This doesn't mean abandoning discernment. Satan masquerades as an angel of light (2 Corinthians 11:14), and not everything supernatural is godly. Not every alleged UFO encounter is pleasant. But the solution isn't denying all extraordinary experience—it's applying biblical tests rigorously.

To those who've had similar experiences but stayed silent: your testimony matters. Not because it proves UFOs are angels, but because it witnesses to the reality that God still works wonders (however that happens), still sends messengers, still intervenes in ways exceeding our categories. You're not alone. You're not crazy. And you're not required to explain everything before acknowledging something extraordinary occurred.

To skeptics who find these accounts unconvincing: I respect your caution. Skepticism has its place. But consider whether your skepticism is truly neutral or whether it's defending a worldview that can't accommodate the experiences described here. Are you evaluating evidence fairly, or explaining it away because it threatens assumptions you're not ready to question?

To believers who worry this book opens dangerous doors: your concern is legitimate. Deception is real. Testing spirits is essential. But fear of deception shouldn't lead us to deny all spiritual experience. That's like refusing to eat because some food is poisoned. The solution isn't abstinence but discernment—learning to recognize what's genuine, what's questionable, what's clearly wrong.

The heavens declare God's glory (Psalm 19:1). Sometimes they do so quietly, through sunsets and star patterns we can predict and photograph. But sometimes—just sometimes—they do so dramatically, through lights that move wrong and presences that feel holy and moments that shatter certainty

Lights in the Sky

that we understand how God works.

I don't claim these stories prove angels pilot craft that look like UFOs. I don't claim all unexplained phenomena are divine. I simply suggest we shouldn't automatically dismiss the possibility, especially when encounters bear good fruit and lead toward rather than away from Christ.

The world is wider than our theologies. Creation is stranger than our science admits. And God is more creative than our categories allow.

Perhaps it's time we expanded our vision, opened our hearts, and acknowledged that reality—especially spiritual reality—exceeds current understanding. The people in this book did exactly that. They encountered mystery, tested it against Scripture, evaluated the fruit, and concluded they'd glimpsed something genuine even if they couldn't explain it fully.

Their humility teaches us. They didn't claim to have all answers. They simply testified: "This happened. It changed me. It pointed me toward God. Make of it what you will."

That testimony deserves hearing. Not uncritical acceptance, but serious consideration. Because if heaven still sends messengers, if angels still minister, if lights still guide and voices still warn and presences still comfort—then we serve a God more active, more present, more engaged with His creation than comfortable Western Christianity often admits.

And if we've been too quick to explain away the extraordinary, too eager to rationalize mystery, too afraid of deception to remain open to genuine encounter—then we've shrunk God to fit our categories rather than expanding our categories to hold God's vastness.

The lights are still appearing. The watchers are still watching. The guardians are still guiding. Not everyone sees them—perhaps not even most people. But those who do are being invited into deeper awareness: that we're not alone, that we're not forgotten, that heaven touches earth in ways both subtle and spectacular.

Some will call these stories dangerous. Others will call them delusional. Still others will recognize in them echoes of their own experiences, finally finding permission to speak what they've witnessed.

To the latter group especially: speak carefully but speak truthfully. The church needs your stories—not to create new doctrine, but to remind us that the God of the Bible still works wonders, still sends messengers, still declares His glory through the heavens.

It's also important pushback against the New Age woo out there and also the modern fear-based theology that insists all UFOs/aliens are demons — an idea that seems mainstream now but would have been left field centuries back.

Maybe it's time we looked up with both reverence and expectation, ready to see the chariots of God wherever they appear—even if they look stranger and more wonderful than we ever imagined.

Knowing God

If you have read these stories, you will have seen a thread running through them: God has never stopped reaching for people. Angels are only one way He whispers, "You are not alone. You are not forgotten."

But the greatest message He ever sent was not through angels, but through His Son, Jesus Christ. Jesus entered our world, took on our pain, died for our sins, and rose again so that nothing—not even death—could separate us from God's love.

The Bible says, "For God so loved the world that He gave His one and only Son, that whoever believes in Him shall not perish but have eternal life" (John 3:16). That promise includes you.

Maybe you don't know God yet, but as you've read these pages, you've sensed that tug on your heart. Maybe you feel the same gentle voice that many in these stories heard: Come home. You are not forgotten.

If so, you don't need perfect words. Jason's four word prayer was enough to be heard. You don't need to clean yourself up first. God asks only for honesty, for a willing heart. If you want to take that step of faith, you can pray something like this:

"Lord Jesus,

> *I believe You love me. I confess I have sinned, and I need Your forgiveness. Thank You for dying for me and rising again. I open my life to You. Be my Savior, my Lord, my friend. From this day on, I choose to follow You. .... Amen."*

If you prayed this prayer sincerely, then welcome—you belong to Him. Heaven rejoices over one who comes home. Find a Bible, connect with a church, and keep walking this journey. You will discover, as countless others have, that you are never alone.

FINAL WORD

If this book has resonated with you—if you've experienced something similar or simply appreciate these stories being told with care and discernment—please consider leaving a review. These testimonies need to be shared, not to create new theology but to encourage those who've been silent too long.

If you have your own story—an encounter with unexplained lights, guidance you can't explain, protection that seemed to come from beyond human help—I'd be honored to hear it. Not every story fits into a book, but every testimony matters. You can reach me through my publisher at info@cosmicjivepublishing.com with **"PASTOR JOE - LIGHTS"** in the subject line.

These stories are precious not because they answer all questions but because they remind us that questions are okay. Mystery is okay. Not knowing doesn't mean it didn't happen. Sometimes the most faithful response to the inexplicable is simply: "I saw something extraordinary. I don't fully understand it. But I know it pointed me toward God. And that's enough."

May you walk with eyes open to wonder, heart ready for mystery, and spirit willing to acknowledge that the heavens still declare His glory—in ways both familiar and impossible to categorize.

The God who made the stars still works through them. The God who created light still manifests in it. The God who sends messengers throughout Scripture still sends them today.

Sometimes they look exactly like we expect. Sometimes they appear in forms that challenge every category we've created.

But they're always doing the same work: pointing us toward the One who sent them, declaring that we're not alone, reminding us that reality is larger and stranger and more beautiful than we dared imagine.

Next book - coming by January 2026!

THE CHARIOTS OF GOD
Christian Testimonies of UFOs, Angels & The Mysterious, Volume 2

ISBN 978-1-918219-08-1

Including missing time and sighting of actual craft (not just lights) followed by sustained paranormal activity.

www.ingramcontent.com/pod-product-compliance
Lightning Source LLC
Chambersburg PA
CBHW030331080526
44584CB00012B/812